The Creative Advantage Life Cycle

Enhance your creativity throughout all stages of your life

BY MARIA SIMONELLI

Other books by this author

The Creative Advantage: How the intersection of science and creativity reveals life's ultimate advantage (2021)

The Creative Advantage: Activity Guide (2021)

Sweet Spot Careers: A Practical and Creative Guide to a Successful Midlife Career Transition (2013)

First published in 2021 by Maria Simonelli

© Maria Simonelli 2021

The moral rights of the author have been asserted

All rights reserved. Except as permitted under the *Australian Copyright Act 1968* (for example, a fair dealing for the purposes of study, research, criticism or review), no part of this book may be reproduced, stored in a retrieval system, communicated or transmitted in any form or by any means without prior written permission.

All inquiries should be made to the author.

Project management by Publish Central

Disclaimer: The material in this publication is of the nature of general comment only, and does not represent professional advice. It is not intended to provide specific guidance for particular circumstances and it should not be relied on as the basis for any decision to take action or not take action on any matter which it covers. Readers should obtain professional advice where appropriate, before making any such decision. To the maximum extent permitted by law, the author and publisher disclaim all responsibility and liability to any person, arising directly or indirectly from any person taking or not taking action based on the information in this publication.

CONTENTS

Chapter 1: Introduction — 5
    A Creative Life Cycle — 7
    Section 1: Recap — 8
    Section 2: Nurturing the Creative Advantage in Children — 8
    Section 3: Cultivating the Creative Advantage in the Workplace — 9
    Section 4: Optimising the Creative Advantage for Well-Being — 9

Section 1: What is the Creative Advantage? — 11

Chapter 2: The Creative Fundamentals — 12
    How do we define creativity? — 12
    Are you a little-c or Big-C creative? — 13
    What's going on in the creative brain? — 14
    The deliberate analysis mode — 14
    The spontaneous insight mode — 15
    The whole brain at work — 15
    Can the brain change? — 17

Chapter 3: Introducing the Four Essential Creative Elements — 19

Section 2: Nurturing the Creative Advantage in Children — 21

Chapter 4: The Role of Parents, Educators and Mentors — 22
    Develop creative thinking skills through reading — 23
    Encouraging group creativity — 23
    Freedom to decide — 24
    Child-centred environments — 24
    Creating innovators — 25
    The role of mentors — 25

Chapter 5: The Power of Play — 28
    What is play? — 29

Chapter 6: Transitioning from Home to School — 31
    Cultivating classroom creativity — 32
    Developing creative capacity in your children — 34
    Reflection – Where can you have the most influence to create an advantage? — 35
    As parents, teachers and mentors we can: — 35
    When seeking preschool and primary schools for children, look for and ask: — 35
    When seeking a senior school experience, ask does the school: — 36

Section 3: Cultivating the Creative Advantage in the Workplace — 37

Chapter 7: Seeking Out Workplace Creativity — 38

    The VUCA world of work   39

    Applying the Creative Elements Model   40

Chapter 8: How the Work Environment Influences Motivation   42

Reflection – Part 1
What work environment factors are important to support your intrinsic motivation?   43

Reflection – Part 2
What do you consider important to support your intrinsic motivation?   45

Assessing an organisation for creativity   46

Reflection – Part 3
What should I look for in a future employer?   47

Chapter 9: Managing Creativity Versus Managing For Creativity   49

What role does management play in fostering the creative process in the workplace?   49

Reflection – Are you managing for creativity?   49

From manager to transformational leader   55

Section 4: Optimising the Creative Advantage for Well-Being   59

Chapter 10: The Significance of Everyday Creativity   60

The intersection of creativity and well-being   63

Reflection – Leverage your advantage to expand your everyday motivation and well-being   65

Chapter 11: Everyday Creativity Through the Arts   66

Crafting a healthier mindset   66

Creative health: innovative approaches to healthcare   67

Utilising the arts to assist learning   70

Reflection – Where can you introduce art and craft into your well-being approach?   71

Chapter 12: Maximising Our Creativity As We Age   73

The changing brain   75

Sustaining creativity as we mature   76

Reflection – Are you a sprinter or marathoner?   77

Creativity is our greatest asset   79

Appendix   81

Who do you think were conceptual or experimental innovators?   81

The Essential Elements to Creativity   82

The Role of Mindset   82

Understanding Deliberate Practice   82

The Top Seven Skills that Make Up a Creative Skill Set   83

Get More Creative Advantage   84

References   86

Endnotes   88

CHAPTER 1

Introduction

Creativity is the most important asset we have to negotiate through this rapidly changing world.

From the way we manage our work life and conduct business, to how we learn a new skill, model behaviours for our children and shape the way we age to express our unique selves, the creative brain has no limits.

By broadening the applicability of creativity and recognising how it can elevate us both personally and professionally, we can start to realise the enormous reach we can have as parents, leaders, educators and in everyday life. We can establish the foundations of the creative advantage.

As leaders we can have more impact as we learn the skills of effective and creative leadership to enable us to manage the challenges faced by our workplace teams, organisations and the society at large.

As educators and parents, we're discovering the role creativity plays in development and learning, with educational psychologists identifying that the creative process underpins classroom learning as well as critical informal learning from speaking our first language to engaging in group play.[1]

As maturing adults we can tap into positive peak experiences, the 'flow' that contributes to happy, healthy and fulfilling lives, as well as face everyday problems that require creative responses.

We must nurture and take advantage of our own individual creative abilities if we're to solve the pressing problems facing our world. This ultimately is the objective of this book, to lay out the science behind the apparent mystery of creativity, to not only appreciate our creative potential but to give us all the motivation and the tools to obtain a creative advantage in all aspects of life.

Neuroscience points to the growing understanding that while most of us may be born with more or less the same brain, our capacity to use it can be strengthened throughout our life by the way we strengthen our creative abilities.

While The Creative Advantage draws on many studies, it notes the important foundation led by Harvard Professor Teresa Amabile, whose work by her team over many years has had a profound impact on the way the topic has been understood, particularly in workplace culture.

What we'll learn from their work is that there are four key elements to achieve creativity. Three of these are internal to us and we have the direct ability to enhance these:

- Intrinsic motivation – our willingness to engage, our mindset and desire to work with challenges
- Domain relevant skills defined by subject-area expertise to draw upon as we progress through a creative process
- Creative process skills and behaviours – while these may vary depending on our personality, they're all conducive to problem-solving.

The fourth element that exists outside the individual is our environment. The family, social environments and our workplaces can have a profound influence, either positivity or negativity, to affect creative expression.[2]

The elegance of this model, that we'll refer to as the *Creative Elements Model*, is that it's applicable across all aspects of our lives. Motivation can be influenced through the design of schools, jobs and through following our curiosity. Domain expertise can be improved through the way we practice, and creative process skills can be learnt. Increasing research into the work environment has led to more awareness of its association with organisational innovation.

The advantage is when you have these elements all working in your favour, they can combine to give you a creative advantage. When supplemented by creative problem-solving tools, you can ensure a creative outcome every time.

The Creative Advantage demonstrates that we're all born to be creative. It's a necessary and innate ability, with an evolutionary basis that natural selection has favoured, to enable us to mix things up to stay on top of what life can throw at us. Like any ability, while we have a certain capacity, we can learn and improve them.

The first book in this series, *The Creative Advantage: How the intersection of science and creativity reveals life's ultimate advantage*, explored this deep dive into the science that fuels creativity, through seven key themes.[3]

Briefly, they were the:

- Creative Fundamentals: The how, what, why and when of creativity
- Creative Elements Model: These are mindset and motivation, domain expertise, creative skill sets and your social and work environment
- Conditions for Creativity: To increase your brain's creative capacity to harness spontaneous insights
- Body-Brain Connection: Recognises that creativity is dependent on your body and brain's health

- Building Creative Routine: Leverage the neuroplasticity behind habits
- Creative Problem-Solving Tools: Learn practical tools for everyday and bigger problem-solving.

Ultimately, creativity is as much about what we do, as it is about how we do it and *The Creative Advantage Life Cycle* reveals how creativity leads to the powerhouse of innovation, helping us all to use these learnings successfully in both our personal and professional lives, to influence organisational cultures and more broadly, society. But creativity is also visible in those seemingly small decisions we make daily, and this 'little-c' everyday creativity can be influenced with the creative techniques outlined in this book series.

It's curated from the latest research from the world's most renowned experts and thinkers in the fields of neuroscience, cognitive psychology, social science, education and psychology to provide an understanding and practical approach to successfully create an advantage where you work, live, play and as you age.

A Creative Life Cycle

A life cycle is defined as the developmental stages that occur during an organism's lifetime.

For us humans, the major stages of the life cycle include pregnancy, infancy, the toddler years, childhood, puberty, older adolescence, adulthood, middle age, and the senior years.

We know that with proper nutrition and exercise, we can ensure good health and mental well-being throughout our lifespan. But where does creativity fit into this? This book explores how we can utilise creativity to proactively enhance every aspect of our life from the early years, schooling and further education, work life, as well as our health and well-being as we age.

While this book is for those seeking ways to express their creativity in all aspects of their life, it's also relevant to those at a crossroad, challenged by juggling roles as parents, combined with a demanding work life and the needs of ageing parents, leaving them somewhat overwhelmed and impacting on their mental and physical well-being. Let's recognise the complexity of modern life and tap into practical creative problem-solving approaches to support us across our lifespan.

This book considers the questions we can ask ourselves that drive the notion of creativity into a distinct advantage, rather than just leaving it to chance.

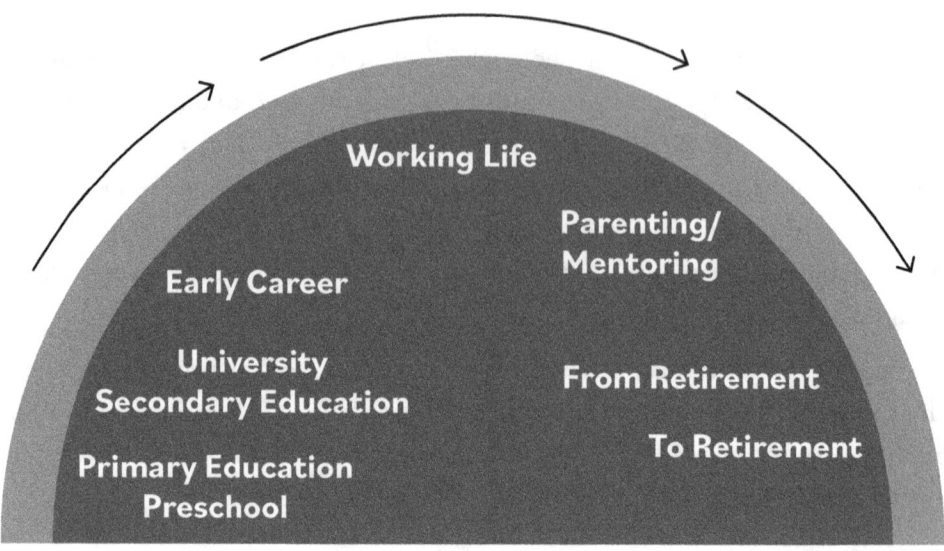

Section 1: Recap

This book starts with a recap on the creative fundamentals, what's going on in the brains of creative people and the essential elements to creativity.

It's then divided into three sections to mirror important life stages:

Section 2: Nurturing the Creative Advantage in Children

Understand the formative roles that parents, educators and mentors have in influencing the development of the creative advantage in children from preschool through to secondary education. Use the creative elements and apply these throughout a child's life, starting with:

- recognising the importance of strong creative role models
- understanding how play and reading shape children's creativity
- developing creative capacity throughout their schooling.

Section 3: Cultivating the Creative Advantage in the Workplace

Learn how to pursue creativity in your workplace, to enhance your own individual skills and the organisation to succeed by:

- identifying workplaces that value creative approaches as a way of supporting staff as well as bringing a unique product and service to the market
- understanding the important role intrinsic motivation plays in our response to creativity in the workplace
- the transformational role managers can play to foster creativity.

Section 4: Optimising the Creative Advantage for Well-Being

Explore the evidence and how to best apply the creative elements to shape and realise a vision for a creative life well lived by:

- highlighting the health and well-being benefits associated with creative art practices
- maximising creativity as we age and its impact on reducing cognitive decline.

My vision is for the reader to unlock the amazing potential that lies within each of you, to demonstrate that once you understand the elements that contribute to creativity, you can transform the way you are in the world. To turn off your autopilot, be actively engaged rather than a passive observer of other's creativity and learn what you can do to live a creative life.

Chapter by chapter, this book will provide both the relevant science, as well as strategies to empower you to pursue new ideas drawn from the best creative thinkers. With new skills and renewed motivation, you can develop the confidence to pursue creativity in all aspects of your life.

SECTION 1

What is the Creative Advantage?[4]

CHAPTER 2

The Creative Fundamentals

We know that creativity cuts across artistic, scientific, business and technology modes; it affects every domain of human enterprise. A creative mind is at work whether it's working on a new recipe, painting a canvas, or creating a theory, strategy, widget or formula. While some creatives wear an art smock and others wear a lab coat, they all bring ideas into the world using similar patterns of development to shape their process.

Everything we see, feel and touch around us has been created by those before us. Ever since humans who look like us, Homo sapiens, first appeared two hundred thousand years ago, they've been creating and innovating. No other species has the capacity to imagine, create change or can claim to be as creative. Some researchers have even said we're hardwired for creativity as it's a deep-seated trait necessary for human survival.[5]

How do we define creativity?

Creativity is the innate quest for originality driven by an enduring human passion for novelty, the discovery of the new, solving of old challenges and the evoking of a new thrill.[6]

The Creative Advantage works with the notion that creativity is on a spectrum that begins with imagination as it progresses to innovation. While the processes and activities of creativity and innovation are similar, they do require an understanding of different approaches.

Creativity is associated with developing new products, services and solutions. It examines unknown areas, connecting ideas to find unique problem-solving approaches and novel ways of performing a task. It can be undertaken by an individual and group and defined as both a process and an outcome.

In defining creativity, firstly, it must be new, novel and original. Its second component is appropriateness; this refers to the value or fit in a given context. Value also refers to ideas being workable, useful or adaptive. So, for a person's achievements, an idea or a product to be considered creative it needs to be new or original and of value.

There are many interpretations of creativity and various ways the term is used. In the 1970s many psychologists argued that creativity and problem-solving were the same thing.[7] But we know that creativity is more than just problem-solving. Sometimes, it's more like problem finding, where we may start a creative process without even knowing what the real problem is, the goal is unclear or the parameters ill-defined.

For consistency this book uses the term 'creativity' as an overarching way to explain a number of concepts. The term is used to describe, as shorthand, cognitive processes including creative thinking, problem-solving and problem finding.[8]

It also includes both the deliberate or spontaneous modes of creativity. For example, many science experiments could be categorised as deliberate cognitive forms of creativity. These are experiments that aim to discover something new, are informed by previous studies or might take trial and error to get to a solution. On the other hand, some scientific discoveries are inspired by more spontaneous moments where the solution seems to come from a sudden insight.[9]

This book also recognises the importance of artistic expression as a practical way to train our brain to see in a unique way. Artistic techniques like drawing, music or dance are valuable in themselves, as they can strengthen our problem-solving approach to strategise and create ways to see the bigger picture.[10]

Neuroscientist Dr Wendy Suzuki, author of *Healthy Brain, Happy Life*, points to studies that have shown a strong link between creativity and positive emotions, so much so they are more likely to have a creative breakthrough.[11]

Creativity has been positively correlated to emotions like joy and curiosity. Art is an amazing medium to take us on a journey through visual, auditory and tactile stimulation. Conversely, negative emotions like fear and anger can also be channelled into a creative outcome. We've often seen people's misfortune channelled into something positive such as a community movement, philanthropic or grassroots organisation. We'll explore more of these ideas as we progress through this book.

Are you a little-c or Big-C creative?

When we think about creativity, we often fall into the trap of comparing ourselves to heavyweight creatives like Amadeus Mozart, Albert Einstein, Steve Jobs or Coco Chanel. They are referred to as 'Big-C' or 'Pro-C' creatives as a way to think about people with well-formed and mature special talents.

A Pro-C creative has used intense deliberate practice within their specific domain to reach their higher level of professional expertise or significant creative accomplishment.[12] But creativity is also evident in other ways, like the way we express our problem-solving in everyday life, referred to as 'little-c' creatives.[13]

Creativity will follow a trajectory that starts with personally meaningful interpretations of experiences, actions and events, that progress to novel and meaningful contributions (what we'll call little-c creativity) and can even develop into superior creative performance (Big-C or Pro-C creativity).[14]

The take-home message is that with all these creative types, they all fundamentally use the same thought processes. The Big-C creatives become great the same way that everybody else does.

What's going on in the creative brain?

Just like artists and corporate leaders, neuroscientists are interested in understanding how we can improve our creative cognitive processes. Creativity can't be simply reduced to the neural circuitry of the brain. Research paints a complex picture of the relationship between brain science and creativity.

Consider what happens when you are confronted with a problem. Do you sit down and analytically work through it, or do you more often just wait for a sudden insight where a solution pops into your head out of mid-air? More often than not, you probably have experienced both. These are the so-called 'analysis versus insight' creative modes.

The analysis mode is also referred to as *deliberate*, while the insightful is referred to as *spontaneous* or the 'aha' mode.[15]

It's uniformly agreed by neuroscience that creativity is a complex and multifaceted construct that we humans demonstrate in many different ways. Most of us will use both methods when tackling problems or bringing creative ideas, products and services to life.

The deliberate analysis mode

The deliberate analysis mode is described as thoughtful and purposeful solving of problems, retrieving knowledge and making plans, often called the higher-order thinking skills. It's the logical, deductive and incremental approach that typically results in a gradual solution of a problem.

It's associated with conscious processing, executive attention, effort, purposeful memory retrieval, intentionality, evaluation and planning. This type of creativity is observed when we ideate and then evaluate ideas by a logical, systematic and conscious reasoning approach.[16]

The spontaneous insight mode

The spontaneous insight mode is characterised by undirected, unintentional thought and associated with imagining the future. It might come after restructuring a problem, followed by the sudden experience where the solution was at least partly or wholly solved.

It's associated with an opposite set of attributes. There's no sense of urgency. It's more about inattention, effortlessness, undirected memory retrieval and unconscious processing. While this unconscious processing also has access to working memory, it also can chance upon remote associations.[17]

Science is filled with stories of innovative revelations where creative flashes came to its creator. Imagine Isaac Newton watching apples fall from a tree that helped inspired him to develop his law of universal gravitation. Or Archimedes 'eureka' moment after he stepped into a bath and noticed the water rise that led him to discover the principle of displacement.

Both these examples occurred while in a relaxed state or daydreaming. While these examples show flashes of insight, they also came to these scientists while working on these problems over a long period of time while displaying highly developed subject expertise and knowledge.

Consciously raising memories of similar situations from the past will influence our assessment of what's happening now. The trick is to introduce a creative problem-solving model to ensure you can counterbalance the possible biases that come from relying solely on your assumptions and memories.

The whole brain at work

Let's learn more about what's actually going on as neuroscientists have begun to uncover the brain regions that are most active during problem-solving and creativity. For a long time, there was a neuro myth that the left logical brain was associated with analytical, critical and mathematical thinking, while the right brain was the artistic, abstract and intuitive side. It's now thought that creativity is not just a right-brain function found in one distinct region of the brain as popularly thought.

These processes are shared across a number of brain regions working together.

Although one brain region may be principally responsible for certain functions, researchers now believe there is more load distribution across the brain structures, demonstrating the brain's ability to share tasks and create a workaround to undertake a task.[18]

Brain scans of people making decisions show many different and apparently unrelated parts of the brain firing at once when they're thinking about a complex problem. Information flows from left to right, back to front and bottom to top. The more agile and healthy the brain, the better this whole-brain connectivity works.[19]

The neuroscience concludes that creative thought comes about by more complex and dense neural connectivity between major regions of the brain.[20] The brain region activated depends on what stage of the creative process you're at, as different regions are recruited at different stages to process different tasks.

In studies conducted where people undertook open-ended problem-solving through divergent thinking, three distinct brain networks were identified: these are the default mode network, the executive control network and the salience network.

These networks are made up of neurons, a nerve cell that is the basic building block of the nervous system, which are specialised to transmit information throughout the body.

The **default mode network** often called the imagination network, is associated with many different types of cognition that involve spontaneous or self-referential thinking. It's called the default mode because it's activated when people are just relaxing, daydreaming or letting their minds wander and imagine ideas.

The **executive control** or cognitive control network is activated when we focus our attention and cognitive resources on more demanding tasks that require us to have higher levels of concentration or where we need to manage multiple things at once. This is where reading, study and mastery of language occur. This network is not engaged for all creative processes or the initial creative process. It's thought to be used in the second stage of creativity, when we are focusing on checking and editing the ideas.

The third network is the **salience network**. It plays an important role in switching between these two neuron networks: idea generation mode, the default process; and the idea evaluation mode, the controlled way of thinking. It's called salience because it helps us to pick up on salient information internally or in the surrounding environment.

Researcher Professor Roger Beaty, from the Cognitive Neuroscience of Creativity

Lab in the US, says that the default mode network and the executive control network typically don't work together.[21]

Observations via a brain scanner show that when one network is activated, the other network tends to deactivate. So, for example, when we're mind wandering, the default network tends to show increased activation and the cognitive control network tends to deactivate. Likewise, when we need to pay close attention and focus on something, this executive control network activates and the default network deactivates.[22]

By tracing the patterns of connections in the brain, Professor Beaty has built a brain network model that predicts which participants in his study are more or less creative.[23] His team has observed that people who show stronger connections between these three different brain networks tend to come up with more original ideas. This reflects the ability to switch between these kinds of spontaneous and controlled modes of thinking.

Their conclusion is that creative people have the ability to switch between, co-activate or exchange information between these three networks, to produce more original ideas. The executive attention network needs to be switched on to identify a problem or define a challenge to get into a problem-solving mode. But this network switches off as the mind wanders and imagines possible solutions in the default mode. In the meantime, the salience network monitors what's going on and assesses the surrounds, before the brain switches back to executive attention mode to help determine the best solution to the challenge at hand.

Can the brain change?

There's a lot of interest in the brain's ability to change or rewire itself through the work of psychiatrist and psychoanalyst Dr Norman Doidge, who has written extensively on the brain's plasticity, referred to as neuroplasticity.[24] From the 1990s onwards, the research into neuroplasticity exploded and brain scans revealed that increased learning can lead to great increases in plasticity and new connections all over the brain.[25] Appreciating the brain's ability to learn helps us to understand the potential for greater creative processes in our lives.

This recent research has shown that under the right circumstances, the power of brain plasticity can help adult minds grow. Although certain brain functions tend to decline with age, there are steps people can take to tap into plasticity and reinvigorate that machinery. These circumstances include focused attention, determination, hard work and maintaining overall brain health.[26]

This is demonstrated by a series of in-depth studies undertaken by Professor Eleanor Maguire, a neuroscientist at University College London, who examined the brain scans of London cab drivers.

London's lack of a grid, one-way streets, traffic circles and dead ends as well as the erratic numbering system, led to many visitors being advised to take a taxi rather than rely on navigational systems in rental cars.

The cabbies are known for being able to get you from point A to point B in the most efficient way due to the need for them to pass a series of exams that test their 'knowledge' of the streets. To master the knowledge, prospective cabbies must master a guidebook through physically travelling various possible routes. The resulting memory and navigational skills have proven to be of great interest to psychologists interested in learning how this intense training affects the brain.

Professor Macquire's work confirmed that a particular part of the hippocampus, the part of the brain that holds spacial representation capacity, was larger in these drivers compared to other subjects, in response to the need to navigate and learn street names and locations. Further, the human brain grows and changes in response to intense training. The years spent mastering the knowledge had enlarged the parts of the brain responsible for navigating from one place to another. The extended practice resulted in the brain's ability to learn, problem-solve and ideate quickly, enabling these drivers to get customers to their destination with the most direct route.[27]

This helps us to understand how the brain can be 'rewired' in response to experiences over a lifetime. While biology provides our neurons at birth, our experience and surrounding environment help to sculpt and wire patterns as we mature into adults. Behaviours will lead to changes in brain circuitry, just as brain circuitry will lead to behavioural change.

The brain can also rewire itself to enable it to deal with the changes required when learning a new skill. While we know its ability to do this varies with age, we also know that the brain with continuous practice, will lay down new neural pathways, increasing the number of circuits and laying down new memory.

The brain can change, as we'll learn, through dedicated practice. Similarly, we can teach an older brain new information to slow age-related mental decline. A lifetime of experiences reorganises the structure of the brain and points to skills we can master to be more creative in all aspects of life.

CHAPTER 3

Introducing the Four Essential Creative Elements

We know what creativity is, why it's important and the enormous capacity of the brain to rewire and learn new skills. Let's explore the four key elements that we have within our power to influence, that all contribute to increasing our creativity.

In this chapter you'll be introduced to the *Creative Elements Model*. This draws on the work of Professor Teresa Amabile from the Harvard Business School, known for her long-term research on creativity.[28] Her team has created a neat theory that helps us to understand the four elements that when aligned can assist us to take full advantage of creating the best creative outcome.

The *Creative Elements Model* provides a unifying model that helps makes sense of the various elements involved in building our internal creative capacity as well as how we might influence the external environment to achieve better creative results. When working together these elements can influence how creative an individual can become. When organisations understand and apply this model, this can support their staff to be their best creative selves.

The Creative Advantage has adapted and deconstructed Professor Amabile's theory, simplified the terms, all to emphasise the key areas that we can directly influence.

There are four components to the model: they are intrinsic task motivation, domain expertise, creativity relevant processes and, an external component, the social or work environment.[29]

Intrinsic motivation explores one's passion, willingness to engage and the desire to solve a problem for the mere challenge and satisfaction of working on it. It's opposite to extrinsic motivators that arise from rewards, competition, evaluation or a requirement to do something in a certain way.

We'll explore the various ways we can encourage intrinsic motivation, as well as creativity as a state of mind through growth and fixed mindsets and how understanding internal motivation can assist to build a creative workplace culture.

Domain expertise is the knowledge, technical skills or talent in an individual's given domain. These are necessary resources, skills and raw materials that individuals will draw upon as they move through the creative process.

We'll focus on the value of deliberate practice to further build these domain skills.[30]

The ***Creativity Relevant Processes*** are the skills or techniques we use to approach a given problem to generate solutions and examine it from various angles, combine our knowledge from multiple fields and depart from status quo responses. They may vary depending on personality characteristics that are conducive to independence, risk-taking and taking new perspectives on problems, as well as a disciplined work style and using tools to generate ideas.

We'll reference the work of Drs Mandell and Jordan from their research published in *Becoming a Life Change Artist*, specifically identifying the skills and behaviours of successful creative types and how we might build these for our everyday use.

The fourth element is the ***Social or the Work Environment***. This element exists outside of the individual. We'll learn that as individuals or organisations, it's the area we can most influence, either positivity or negativity, to affect our creative expression.

The key aspects of this model are referred to throughout this book.[31]

The Creative Elements Model[32]

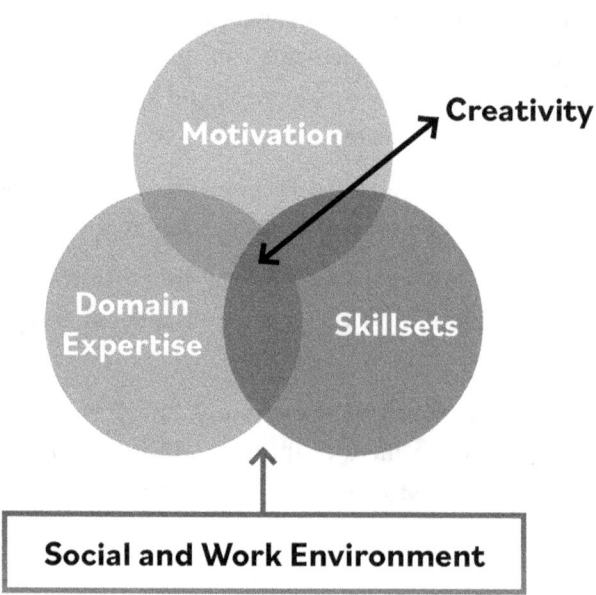

Let's now explore what our life would look like if we reframed the way we approach the significant milestones with a more creative enhancing mindset. As you progress through these chapters, we'll work through the advantages in turn, looking at the science that underpins each and strategies to maximise their creative potential in your life.

SECTION 2

Nurturing the Creative Advantage in Children

We start with the ecosystems surrounding young people and the role parenting, education and mentoring can have to build the creative advantage. Let's explore how to intentionally develop creative, entrepreneurial and innovative skills and talents of young people, to nurture their curiosity and imagination, as well as their analytical problem-solving abilities.

As teachers and/or parents the challenge is to use this important time in a young person's life to build the skills needed to find meaningful careers, become economically independent, at the same time as identifying their own unique talents, to help them shape their own futures and foster a life with purpose and meaning … Sounds so simple!

CHAPTER 4

The Role of Parents, Educators and Mentors

What can parents, educators and mentors do to influence the development of the creative advantage in children from preschool through to secondary education? There are many excellent parenting advice books and websites, so this book won't focus on this important topic. Instead, it points to the research that supports parenting and education practices that contribute to the development of children's creativity.

Whether it's expressed through painting, making or leadership, every parent hopes their child will display some form of creativity. Children who are encouraged to think creatively also have higher self-esteem and intrinsic motivation.[33]

Studies have confirmed that cultivating a children's creative side does correlate with greater professional success later in life, whether or not the child goes into a typically creative profession.

Psychologist and educator Ellis Paul Torrance, known as the 'father of creativity', developed a number of longitudinal studies dating back to the 1950s that followed children through to adulthood.

One study surveyed the creativity of four hundred children through a series of measures that found those with higher creativity scores as children, were more likely in adulthood to have more books published, artworks exhibited, songs composed, ad campaigns executed, research papers published, patents filed and lectures given. The correlation between childhood creativity and adult accomplishment was three times as strong as that between childhood IQ and adult accomplishment.[34]

Nurturing creativity begins with valuing it, reflecting this in the choices we make that encourage self-expression and in how this is modelled in our actions through perspectives shared with children.

As a means to think about how we can foster this, let's refer back to the creative elements model to see how we can develop creative thinking skills, expertise and motivation all within an environment that supports creativity with children.

Develop creative thinking skills through reading

It's well understood that reading is critically important to develop a child's intelligence and boost creativity through exercising their imagination. Let's consider the value of developing creative thinking skills through making reading a ritual.

There's a critical level of literacy required to accumulate knowledge and, for the most part, children get their creative ideas from reading. Adam Grant, psychologist and author of *The Originals*, points to research that could predict patent rates twenty to forty years later by looking at what children's books were popular in a given era: 'If you wanted to know how many patents we would generate in the US today, we should go back to the 1980s and '90s and look at the children's books that were dominant'.[35]

Look no further than entrepreneur Elon Musk, founder of PayPal, Space X and Tesla, as a case study on how reading encourages creativity and innovation. He has been quoted as reading as a child up to ten hours of science fiction a day across a diverse array of subjects. He says books played a crucial role in fuelling his ambitions and coming up with creative solutions to a number of problems facing modern society.[36]

Further research has shown that reading can boost mental capacity by improving brain function through measurable changes in brain connectivity. The brain activity varies with the peaks and troughs of the story, giving credence to the saying 'reading exercises the brain'. The study also found that reading fiction improves one's ability to empathise and mentally put oneself in the character's shoes.[37]

Providing a variety of books encourages imagination and understanding of the world. Reading to children who then often enact mini-dramas based on stories, becomes another expression of play for children. Continuing to encourage children to read on their own as they get older is also essential, as the discipline of reading develops concentration muscles as well as the habit of self-motivated learning.[38]

Encouraging group creativity

Thinking back to the myths surrounding creativity, the lone creator comes to mind. There is a tendency to attribute breakthroughs to a sole person, ignoring the many influences behind the scenes. However, we know that big creative breakthroughs are more often achieved through collaboration and teams. Teaching children that being able to get along with others by understanding the value of different perspectives and diverse interactions has a big role to play in both creativity and the resulting innovation.

There's growing pedagogic research that argues for creativity, creative thinking, communication and collaboration to be encouraged by parents and taught in kindergartens and early childhood development to support learning foundations as children transition to school.[39]

Freedom to decide

The research on autonomy shows relevance from childhood to adulthood. A study on task autonomy in preschoolers aged between two and six, separated them into two groups. Both groups were asked to make a collage with the first group given the ability to choose the materials to use and the second group given no choice in materials. The collages created were judged for creativeness by professional artists, and the first group were judged significantly more creative. The researchers concluded that the freedom to select their own materials contributed to these collages being more creative.[40]

Child-centred environments[41]

Education is often understood as the sole responsibility of parents and teachers. The Reggio Emilia preschool approach identifies a third teacher between child, teacher and parent: *the environment.*

The Reggio Emilia philosophy places attention on how space can be thoughtfully arranged to provide a key source of educational provocation and insight. By seeing the environment as an educator, its proponents believe the surroundings can be used imaginatively, contributing to children's learning.

While this is not a new concept, the Reggio Emilia schools provide vibrant examples of learning environments that are designed to dazzle the senses and invite curiosity and discovery. Unlike a typical classroom, their walls are not covered with alphabet letters. They're more likely to have posted bulletin board displays and labels on every shelf and surface.

Its approach to teaching and learning draws deeply on how young children perceive and use space to create meaning. They advocate that teachers pay close attention to the myriad of ways in which space can be made to engage, speak and invite interaction. This can be through 'provocations' meant to surprise children, spark discussion and pique their curiosity.

From using aromatic scents to tantalise the children's sense of smell when they first enter the classroom, to bringing in realistic colourful shaped objects for children to use in their play, or by storing colourful objects like buttons and markers in transparent containers, children learn to sort by colour or texture.

Teachers will also listen closely to children's conversations as they engage with their surroundings and use what they hear, see and think about to plan their next activity, one that will build on as well as deepen the children's interest and investigation.

While not as widely known as Montessori or the Waldorf education methods, it's focused strictly on early childhood education and doesn't provide formal credentialed teacher training. The idea is that teachers and parents take the concepts learnt by observation and interaction with Reggio Emilia and incorporate them into their classrooms.

Creating innovators

Educator and author Tony Wagner identified a familiar pattern in the development of young innovators in his book *Creating Innovators*. He interviewed parents of successful young adults to examine the factors that developed the creative capacities of their children.

He found these parents consistently encouraged their children to:

- find and pursue their passions
- figure out how to entertain themselves with a combination of outdoor, nature-based and unstructured time
- find an interest through free form playtime to discover, explore and experiment
- have structured time and clear rules related to reading time (that was not school-related), screen time and bedtime
- understand and calculate risks through unstructured and unsupervised play
- undertake activities outside of the school environment.

Wagner concluded that a childhood of creative play leads to deep-seated interests, which in adolescence and adulthood blossom into a deeper purpose for career and life goals.[42]

The role of mentors

Parents are not alone in influencing their children, and studies are showing the important foundational impact mentors can play in how children express their creativity and originality. Psychologists measuring the influence of parents and mentors had on graduates to determine who had the greatest influence on their lives, noted mentors accounted for a high percentage. Parents can nurture values but, at some point, people need to find their own role models for originality, creativity and inspiration in their own chosen fields.[43]

Finding the right mentor for children could come from many sources, like the stories and biographies of great innovators and inventors throughout history or fictional characters in their most loved novels, where protagonists exercise their creativity in pursuit of adventure.

Author Adam Grant says it's possible that these stories even help to elevate a child's aspirations opening their minds to unconventional paths:

> When asked to name their favourite books, Elon Musk and Peter Thiel, (entrepreneurs and co-founders of PayPal) chose *Lord of the Rings*, the epic tale of a hobbit's adventures to destroy a dangerous ring of power. Sheryl Sandberg (Facebook CEO) and Jeff Bezos (Founder and CEO of Amazon) both pointed to *A Wrinkle In Time*, in which a young girl learns to bend the laws of physics and travel through time. Mark Zuckerberg (Founder and Chair of Facebook) was partial to *Ender's Game*, where it's up to a group of kids to save the planet from an alien attack.[44]

The research also has quantified the powerful effect that mentoring has on young people, with studies pointing to the improved academic, social and economic prospects, that can ultimately strengthen our community. A US national report called *The Mentoring Effect*, demonstrated that young people who were at risk for not completing high school but who had a mentor were 55 per cent more likely to be enrolled in college than those who did not have a mentor.

They were also:

- 81 per cent more likely to report participating regularly in sports or extracurricular activities
- 78 per cent more likely to volunteer regularly in their communities
- More than twice as likely to say they held a leadership position in a club or sports team.[45]

In Sir Ken Robinson's book *The Element*, he points to the four roles mentors serve:[46]

- The first is *recognition*, to assist in identifying skills that others may not have noticed, in particular with a focus on valuing the diversity of our individual talents and aptitudes.
- The second role is *encouragement*, where mentors lead us to believe that we can achieve something that seemed improbable and counsel us through self-doubt.

- The third role is *facilitating* by offering advice and techniques, standing by us when we falter and helping us to recover and learn from mistakes.
- The fourth role is *stretching* to push us past our limits, while they remind us that our goal is never to be average at our pursuits.

Mentors take a unique and personal role in our lives … they open doors and get directly involved in our journeys. They show us the next steps and encourage us to take them.[47]

IQ test versus creative thinking test

Psychologist and educator Ellis Paul Torrance believed creativity should be taught in classrooms. He critiqued the well-known IQ (intelligence quota) test by questioning how it could measure originality when it only sought to measure achieving one correct answer. He believed the IQ test could never identify qualities of creative intelligence such as idea fluency, mental flexibility, originality and idea elaboration. When designing his creative thinking test, he looked to measure skills in producing ideas, shifting perspectives and making novel connections.

His research team tracked these tested children and revisited them twenty, forty and even fifty years later. After the initial study, they discovered that the IQ test undertaken was a poor predictor of creative achievement and no guarantee of a person's ability to produce new and useful work. The Torrance Test was 300 per cent more likely to predict the number of inventions, discoveries and artistic accomplishments achieved in adulthood.[48]

Creative parenting or benign neglect[49]

Tom Kelley, author of *Creative Confidence* and partner with IDEO reflects on his and his brother David's upbringing in an interview undertaken at Google:

> Just thinking about our parents, it wasn't that they were artists … it wasn't that they got out the finger paints with us every day. It was that they gave us a lot of space to do things, they weren't quick to judge us or reign us in when we got a little creative. David and I took a lot of stuff apart as kids, including the family piano and many of those things never went back together … and the parents never complained. It's permission to misbehave a little bit, permission to be creative … and you have this sort of nurturing environment that says it's still going to be okay.

CHAPTER 5

The Power of Play

> Human beings are arguably the most exploratory species ... unlike any other species we create our own environments ... Imagination and creativity are essential to our success. We have to imagine how new places we explore, and the new places we build, will work. – Alison Gopnik[50]

We know that humans are born with an innate sense of curiosity, and we take it for granted that young children will play and pretend in fantasy worlds. While we've assumed that play helps children learn, the last decade of research by cognitive scientists is explaining the importance of play and make-believe.

From an evolutionary perspective, play is ubiquitous and it's not just found with young humans but also with young chimps, wolves, dolphins, rats, crows and even octopuses. Play is especially common in social animals like us, who have relatively long childhoods, parental investment and large brains.[51]

Professor of Psychology, Associate Professor of Philosophy and author Alison Gopnik, studies how babies and young children's minds work. She has undertaken research to show the positive relationship between children's reasoning, thinking about different possibilities and how this helps children learn:

> We've found out that even very young children can already consider possibilities, distinguish them from reality and even use them to change the world. They can imagine different ways the world might be in the future and use them to create plans ... most dramatically they can create completely imaginary worlds, wild fictions and striking pretences ... Children's brains create casual theories of the world, maps of how the world works ... and these theories allow children to envisage new possibilities and to imagine and pretend the world is different.[52]

Professor Gopnik believes that the value of play and make-believe is that it helps children consider what would happen if the world were different, and then working out the consequences. But she stresses that it's the very silliness of play, is what makes it so effective as it teaches us how to deal with the unexpected:[53]

> The idea is that children at play are like pint-sized scientists testing theories. They imagine ways the world could work and predict the pattern of data that would follow if their theories were true, and then compare that pattern with

the pattern they actually see. Even toddlers turn out to be smarter than we would have thought if we ask them the right questions in the right way.[54]

What is play?[55]

Professor Gopnik says biologists who try to define animal play, point to these five distinctive characteristics:

> *Play is not work.* It may look like fighting or hunting, digging or sweeping, but it doesn't actually accomplish anything. The kitten doesn't really eat the string and the wrestling rat doesn't actually hurt his brother, just as playing house doesn't leave the living room any neater.
>
> *While it doesn't actually accomplish anything, isn't just incompetent work.* It has special characteristics that let you distinguish it from the real thing. When rats play fight, they nuzzle each other's necks; when it's for real, they bite each other's flanks. When children pretend to pour tea, they make big exaggerated sloshing movements.
>
> *Play is fun*, even for animals. Babies giggle contagiously over peek-a-boo and rats laugh when they play fight, making a distinctive ultrasonic chirp.
>
> *Play is voluntary.* It's something that an animal does for its own sake, not because it's instructed or rewarded for doing it. In fact, young rats will actually work in order to get to play – they will learn to press a bar that lets them play. But play is not like other basic drives, as animals only play freely when their other basic needs are satisfied. When an animal is starved or stressed, play diminishes.
>
> *Play has a special structure*, a pattern of repetition and variation. When rats play fight, they try different patterns of offense and defence against each other. When a six-month-old plays with a rattle, she tries shaking it louder or softer, banging it against the table with more or less vigour.

Do devices fuel or stunt creativity?[56]

We can't discuss nurturing children's creativity without acknowledging the modern-day elephant in the room ... the growing body of evidence that excessive use of smart devices can have on children's development. From smartphones to tablets, these ubiquitous devices have been associated with decreasing attention spans, higher rates of depression and anxiety and screen addiction.

But do they also affect children's ability to be creative?

Developmental behaviour professor Jenny Radesky, says the lack of studies focused on creativity and child development means there are still many unknowns.[57] What we do know is that screens take children away from unstructured play, outdoor time and daydreaming, which would impact on a child's ability to create visual imagery. She says games like Minecraft are essentially plot-free games where virtual cities can be built. But how does this compare with making an actual 3D Lego city? These apps also force children to play by the developer's rules rather than allowing a child to have an original idea to explore and run with.

While we know there needs to be limits on what children are viewing and for how long, we also need to consider the positive aspects of digital technology and how it can enhance creativity. Do the apps and games lead them to recall information, build literacy, be more imaginative after they shut down the device and take the learnings into the real world?

She concludes that rather than a focus on which devices children are using and for how long, we should be asking another question. Instead, ask what content they're viewing and does this engage them in creative expression?

CHAPTER 6

Transitioning from Home to School

> Ironically, in a society that values creativity and innovation more and more, we provide fewer and fewer unfettered opportunities for children to explore.
> – Alison Gopnik[58]

There's a growing chorus of education experts advocating to ensure that playtime is maintained as part of play-based learning, especially in preschool, but also as children transition to primary school.

They're calling for secure time for unstructured, spontaneous activities, particularly with outdoor play and the need to gently prepare children for this transition.

These advocates are responding to studies showing that some young children commencing school are not developmentally ready. They're presenting with higher levels of emotional problems linked to anxiety, depression and physical complaints.[59] Research professor Dr Peter Gray, points to growing rates of psychopathology in children and adolescents associated with the trend for less free play and recess time, as well as with more structured activities taking over family lifestyles. He believes that anxiety and depression relate to people's lack of control over their own lives.

Self-directed play can provide children with some charge of their own destiny, enabling them to learn how to make decisions and develop an internal locus of control.[60] Two play types have been the primary focus of studies that examined the benefits of play-based learning. The first is free play, which is directed by the children themselves, is voluntary, internally motivated and pleasurable.

The next is guided play, which is play that has some level of teacher guidance and aims to embed learning opportunities into the play itself. Both forms, to varying degrees, can develop social and emotional competencies, academic learning and collaboration.[61]

Play-based learning extends into other developmental areas with results showing that play can strengthen neural pathways associated with learning, enhance well-being, improve memory and organisational abilities. It also teaches children self-regulation, problem-solving skills and encourages creativity and critical thinking.[62]

The power of play is also reinforced by research undertaken by paediatricians to demonstrate that developmentally appropriate play enhances brain and executive function (that is, the process of learning, rather than the content), which allow children to pursue goals and ignore distractions. At a time when early childhood programs are pressured to add more didactic components and less playful learning, they promote the importance of playful learning for healthy child development.[63]

In the same vein, to highlight the importance of play, the UN Convention on the Rights of the Child recognises play as every child's right.[64]

Cultivating classroom creativity

This book is not a thesis on whether the entire education system is or is not working at its best. But it's fair to say that the current system, particularly in secondary education, has suffered from assumptions about what creativity is and a lack of how to teach skills associated with creativity, problem-solving and collaboration that will assist young people to meet the challenges they'll face. We can't continue to ask for future creative and innovative thinkers to join the workforce and yet stifle the very processes that are most likely to develop these skills in students. Why are we seeing a system that in many ways is not responding to a demand for increased creativity competencies?

Education of our young people is part of a system that was largely based on a set of assumptions that no longer exist. We've thankfully moved on from the limited nineteenth-century view that formal education was for the privileged few and developed primarily to meet the needs of the Industrial Revolution for conformity and standardisation.[65]

But in a world where we have the information powerhouse of the World Wide Web at our fingertips, what's the role that education plays? Is it to impart knowledge or nurture curiosity, problem-solving skills and a love of lifelong learning? Creativity expert Professor Gerrard Puccio says the focus should be on teaching students higher-order creative thinking skills from kindergarten to graduate school to adequately prepare them for the future.[66]

Over the past few decades, studies show children's creativity tends to decrease with age with a decline most significant from kindergarten to grade three.[67] It's partly attributed to the increased use of standardised tests, thought to foster conventional linear thinking with less tolerance of divergent thinking skills. This emphasis continues throughout schooling and continues to define the type of thinking required during exams.

Sir Ken Robinson, an education advisor, believes one of the reasons schools are failing is their focus on curriculum and assessment, specifying content and national systems of testing. He also points to the quality of teaching and the need to support teachers, 'whose creative instincts are curbed by standardised education and whose effectiveness is diminished as a result'.[68]

Professor Gopnik agrees and says that there are many good models of enquiry-based education that understand learning happens when children are playing and exploring. Research shows that standardised tests are not able to capture the value of a child's play or exploration, that's enabling them to be creative and learn resilience.[69]

Some creativity advocates think we need a complete overhaul of the education systems from classroom design to curriculum requirements. While others suggest, at least in the short term, we should work with the current system and make creativity a deliberate part of every lesson and subject.[70]

After all this is said, Ken Robinson is still optimistic about what the future of education looks like:

> There is boundless energy amongst teachers ... and more people are looking for alternatives. If you give people permission ... and remove penalties, my experience has always been that people rise to the challenge.[71]

Has Finland designed the perfect education system?

It's not all bad news, with a growing number of examples of schools teaching creativity through both an unstructured and a structured process. Author Tony Wagner in *Creating Innovators* looks to Finland as an example of a country that has made a radical shift in forty years from a comparatively poor country with an agrarian economy and an underperforming education system.

Finland transformed its entire education system to develop the capacities of its young people and the results are demonstrated in the countries innovation rankings. They're now consistently at the top of the OECD international assessment and ranked one of the most innovative countries in the world.[72]

As Wagner (2012) explains:

> Today, Finnish students start school one year later, do less homework, and have a shorter school day and year than students in most developed countries, and the country does not administer any tests for accountability.[73]

Reasons attributed to this turnaround are that Finland has:

- transformed the teaching profession through a radical overhaul of their teacher preparation programs. Teachers are drawn from the top 10 per cent of graduates, all have master's degrees in education funded by the state and are generously renumerated.

- pared down the curriculum to a few concepts that are deeply understood, rather than a fact and test-based curriculum.
- placed a high value on career and technical education in their upper secondary schools (grades ten to twelve) and post-secondary offerings (45 per cent of all high school students choose a technical career versus an academic path).
- emphasised students learn independently and make choices about what they study.
- embraced innovations in teaching and learning at every level.[74]

What this looks like is an education system:
- where teachers have more autonomy including responsibility for assessing students
- there's very little homework and children of all abilities are taught together
- where there is free preschool with an emphasis on emotional development, learning by interacting with others with an emphasis on play.

Creativity starts early and is considered the key behind the country's success with a deeply rooted mindset that student-led discovery and finding their own way to do things leads to better outcomes.[75] Finnish schools are also undergoing an ambitious national redesign and refurbishment of physical buildings using a more open-plan creative design with more flexible educational spaces and acoustics in mind.[76]

What Finland has done is create an education system that reflects what they value. It demonstrates an example of an education system that has at its core the fundamental importance of building creative competency.

Developing creative capacity in your children

Where does this leave the parents and educators convinced that increased teaching based on exploration and creativity is essential? How are the twenty-first century teaching and learning challenges posed by the education system to be tackled?

We can, as Ken Robinson promotes, advocate for real change to rethink the education systems. We can get involved in policy discussions that require teachers, governments and families to all be on the same page in order to progress key arguments.[77]

Equally, we can support teachers who are experimenting with innovative teaching methods to foster greater creativity in their classrooms. Professor Gopnik believes we can assess schools and teachers by how well they educate children, not on how well a child does on a test:

> We could visit classrooms and score the quality of teaching and learning that goes on there, including ... whether the teacher responds differently to different kinds of students, rather than relying on a single test score.[78]

Teachers can also reflect on and be aware of their own biases. While some say they enjoy having creative students in their class, that is until these same children behave impulsively or are nonconformist. Rather than get labelled as troublemakers, these children quickly learn instead to get with the program, keeping their original ideas to themselves.[79]

Reflection – Where can you have the most influence to create an advantage?

As parents, teachers and mentors we can:

- Help children to focus on asking the right questions rather than a memorisation-based multiple-choice approach
- Encourage design-based learning where we define the problem rather than work with predetermined problems
- Tolerate failure and encourage risk-taking and at all stages of educational learning
- Allow more time for students to work collaboratively on interdisciplinary projects that they are actually interested in.

When seeking preschool and primary schools for children, look for and ask:

- What are the values that the learning culture is based around and how do they demonstrate this? Is it collaborative, multidisciplinary learning with thoughtful risk-taking, discovery through trial and error, creatively seeking to leverage intrinsic motivation?[80]
- Does it integrate the importance of play into the curriculum? Are there play options with both structured and unstructured time allocated? Is the play outdoors and even better can they engage with nature?
- Do the playgrounds encourage spaces for thinking and discovery, spaces for activities where moderate risks can be taken and spaces for embracing their senses?[81]
- How does it reward creative behaviour and original self-expression in children?

Returning to the *Creative Elements Model*, how might the four factors that influence creativity be considered in this context and which should be prioritised to create a culture of creativity for students? Researcher and author Professor Amabile presented an interesting disruptive view that of all three internal elements, motivation is far more important than either expertise or skills. She explains: 'Expertise and creative thinking are an individual's raw materials – his or her natural resources. But a third factor – motivation – determines what people actually do'.[82]

Tony Wagner's interviews with both young innovators and their influential teachers and mentors downplay the importance of content expertise. While not suggesting that mastering academic content is not important, they stress the ability to apply this knowledge. The knowledge provides the foundation for continuous learning and problem-solving, but how this content is utilised is more important than the content itself. He goes further to observe the greater importance of creative thinking skills, the role that intrinsic motivation and a sense of purpose all contribute to making the difference to the young adults as they moved from school and university to the workforce.[83]

When seeking a senior school experience, ask does the school:

- Reward individual competition and achievement above teamwork?
- Focus on traditional academic classes organised to communicate and test very specific subject content versus problem-based, multidisciplinary approaches?
- Offer motivational incentives, namely extrinsic incentives such as grades and/or intrinsic incentives such as exploration, empowerment and even play?

In preparing senior students for what they'll encounter in the workforce, reflect on what the school culture can do to influence this through the values, beliefs and behaviours they promote.

When choosing children's schools let's consider our willingness to seek tangible indicators that demonstrate they encourage teamwork, interdisciplinary problem-solving, intrinsic drivers and a kind of empowerment to give individual's confidence to take risks.[84]

Nurturing, developing and optimising children's creativity, enabling them to navigate the complex world they've entered is the least we can do to prepare them for the jobs that haven't even been invented.

SECTION 3

Cultivating the Creative Advantage in the Workplace

CHAPTER 7

Seeking Out Workplace Creativity

Try this little exercise: Google 'workplace creativity'. At the time of writing this book, the search responded with over 68 million hits. Google 'workplace innovation' and this resulted in a staggering 228 million hits.

As the field of creativity research has increased, the area of organisational creativity has especially expanded. As creativity is defined as both a process as well as an outcome, and can be undertaken by literally anyone, it makes sense that business interest and subsequent research would increase. It's not just a reference point for art, as Professor Amabile's research can attest, it's now considered a research domain in its own right, with university business schools at Harvard and neuroscientists at Stanford dedicated to this topic.[85]

At this stage an assumption is being made that you appreciate the benefits of creativity and are wishing to pursue this further in your workplace – either because you're convinced it will enhance your own individual skills and enable you to improve your expertise to achieve at work, or you accept that a workplace that encourages creativity, harnessing the creative abilities of a team, is more likely to facilitate ideas and solutions, enabling both you and the organisation to succeed.

Given there are thousands of books, journals, websites and universities dedicated to providing advice on the value of creative and innovative organisations, this chapter will focus on identifying what to look for in a creative organisation as a means for you to gain a professional creative advantage.

Whether you're seeking to enhance your current role or a new role, this section will help you match the theory with the practice by

- ◈ highlighting the indicators that show an organisation is taking creativity seriously
- ◈ identifying what you need to encourage your own creative skills
- ◈ guiding managers to foster a more creative workplace environment.

The VUCA world of work

As well as death and taxes, the other thing we can be certain of in life ... is change. VUCA is a managerial acronym to describe the *volatile, uncertain, complex* and *ambiguous* nature of business.

Its aim is to emphasis the volatile characteristics of instability and speed of change, information gaps and unpredictability of the future leading to uncertainty, the overwhelming and complex nature of relationships and information, and the lack of clarity or the unknown unknowns leading to ambiguity.

It characterises the world of work, as for many of us we'll no longer have a lifelong career in one role, job and even discipline as it's no longer realistic because of the nature and pace of this change. We can already see this with the growth of contract work in a gig economy leading to the need for adaptive and flexible work approaches.

This changing environment is also asking workers to take greater responsibly for their employability through continuous learning, via informal approaches, stretch work, networking, mentoring and accumulating a portfolio of portable skills.

Employers expect young people to act as intrapreneurs by taking ownership of their roles, working cooperatively and actively adding value to an organisation. An example is seen with the hiring procedure of Google, the world's most highly ranked innovation company. According to their director of talent, they look for intellectual curiosity, a bias towards action and a problem finder. They prize collaboration and the ability to recognise and learn from others with different kinds of expertise.

Given the world of work is facing an even increasingly VUCA environment, what does this mean for creativity? Large corporations recognise that some problems can be solved by following what's been done before. But, more often than not, particularly when the issue is something the organisation hasn't faced before, genuine creative thinking and innovation are needed to satisfy both customers, shareholders and stakeholders.

My own 2016 study on understanding organisational creativity in small- to medium-sized enterprises (SMEs) concluded that while limited by resources, people and finances, SMEs know that to stay competitive, creativity and innovation are vital if the sector is to grow and thrive. Creativity and innovation are no longer buzzwords for the more adventurous large corporations to pursue. Instead there's growing recognition that these approaches are fundamental to any proactive organisation. Organisational creativity is rapidly growing in importance, particularly as it's positively associated with the role that stimulating and supportive workplace environments play.[86]

But we're not just seeking out organisations that believe creativity sits in marketing, research, development and definitely not in accounting. We're looking for the ones that know that creativity can benefit every function of the organisation and this is represented in the culture, seen in the leadership behaviours and even found in the ubiquitous mission statement.

Applying the Creative Elements Model

This is a good time to revisit the four key ingredients of the *Creative Elements Model* and consider how the workplace can foster the internal and external environmental components. While three of the factors are internal, how might the workplace support their enhancement and what role can the social or work environment have to influence creative expression?

Domain Expertise encompasses everything that a person knows and can do in their broad domain. For example, a scientist working in a pharmaceutical company would have a basic talent for thinking scientifically as well as technical skills in biochemistry, medicine and biology. Their expertise could have been acquired and developed further through formal study, practical experience, interaction with other professionals or clients.

Domain expertise is also about making connections, seeing relationships and crossing the boundaries of subject domains. As designer Clement Mok (2005) writes:

> The next ten years will require people to think and work across boundaries into new zones that are totally different from their areas of expertise. They will not only have to cross those boundaries, but they will also have to identify opportunities and make connections between them.[87]

Creative skills and behaviours look at how a person approaches creative thinking, problems and their capacity to put existing ideas together into new combinations and connections. This depends to some extent on personality and how the person thinks and works.

With our scientist example, it could be displayed with how comfortable the person is challenging ideas with colleagues, their flexibility in seeking solutions from other disciplines and overall perseverance in problem-solving. From a workplace perspective, both expertise and creative thinking could be fostered with the addition of time and funds to attend scientific seminars and professional conferences, or training in areas like diagnostic thinking.

As noted earlier, Professor Amabile says of her own model that while expertise and creative thinking are clearly important, it's the third factor of **motivation** that determines what people will actually do. Our scientist might have outstanding educational qualifications and a great facility to generate new perspectives to entrenched problems, but unless they're motivated to act, the expertise and creative thinking will go untapped or be applied to something else.

Professor Amabile's studies show there are two types of motivation: *extrinsic and intrinsic*.

Extrinsic motivation comes from outside a person, whether it be a carrot or a stick and we see it commonly used in the workplace. In our scientist example, this could be using external motivation with something desirable, for example, a financial reward for success, or something painful, like a demotion for failure. While this reward-penalty approach doesn't necessarily stop someone from being creative, growing evidence is showing that it doesn't help either.[88]

Besides financial incentives, performance can also be rewarded by providing public recognition such as through companywide programs or private recognition through manager and employee conversations. Research is showing that recognition can significantly improve the level of innovativeness in people's work output as well as the perception of the culture of the organisation.[89]

When extrinsic and intrinsic motivation combine synergistically they can enhance each other, for example, in the workplace by combining staff reward and recognition for creative ideas through constructive feedback and clearly defined goals with their own internal motivation.[90]

When people are intrinsically motivated, they engage in their work for the sheer challenge, satisfaction and enjoyment of it, rather than by external factors or pressures. Their motivation and thus behaviours can be significantly more enduring than extrinsic motivation.

Maintaining your own creativity in your work depends on maintaining your intrinsic motivation, so that means you should do what you love by finding work that matches with your expertise, your creative skills and your strongest intrinsic motivations. You should also love what you do and that's a matter of finding a work environment that will allow you to retain that intrinsic focus, while supporting your exploration of new ideas.[91]

CHAPTER 8

How the Work Environment Influences Motivation

The research clearly shows that the work environment has a significant effect on a person's level of intrinsic motivation, which in turn affects that person's creativity. This chapter will focus on a number of reflective activities that aim to identify your preferences in regard to workplace culture and the intrinsic motivators that you, consciously or not, respond to.

Author David Burkus believes that an organisation's work environment is the most important and hardest creative element to design for, as it can enhance or detract from creativity by influencing the other three internal components. He notes the:

- organisation's commitment to continuous improvement and learning has a direct effect on the ease with which individuals seek to grow their expertise
- amount of cross-functional work within an organisation affects whether individuals can benefit from the broader group expertise
- openness of top management to new ideas and availability of resources affects how often creative relevant processes are undertaken
- senior management's approach to continuous innovation, whether it's reinforced with actions and policies, all determine how staff express their creativity.[92]

Let's begin by exploring the *psychosocial environment*. This refers to the atmosphere in your workplace, home or classroom and whether it has a positive or negative impact on your feelings, attitudes and behaviours. Researcher Goran Ekvall has studied the relationship between this environment and creativity and came up with ten dimensions that he predicted can influence the levels of creativity experienced.[93]

Reflection – Part 1
What work environment factors are important to support your intrinsic motivation?

Let's reflect on the work environments you experience now, or have in the past, to help identify whether this experience reflects an environment that promotes creative thinking.[94]

Consider the following and rate if your responses are low, medium or high:

Challenge and Meaningfulness

In a high challenge climate, people are intrinsically motivated to make contributions, and find joy and meaningfulness in their work and invest much energy.

- To what degree are you engaged in the work?
- To what degree do you find purpose in what you do?
- Are you stimulated by what you do?

Freedom and Autonomy

In a climate with a large amount freedom, people are given autonomy to define much of their own work. People are able to exercise discretion in their day-to-day activities, and people take the initiative to acquire and share information. In a low freedom environment, everything is prescribed to you.

- Are you able to determine how you'll carry out your work?

Idea Support

In the supportive climate, ideas and suggestions are received in an attentive and kind way by bosses and workmates. People listen to each other and encourage initiatives. Possibilities for trying out new ideas are created and the atmosphere is constructive and positive.

- When an idea is put forward, is it listened to in a generous way?
- Is there a sense of openness to receiving ideas, or is there a concern for sharing ideas and how they'll be reacted to by others including your managers?

Trust and Openness

When there's a strong level of trust, everyone in the organisation dares to put forward ideas and opinions. Initiatives can be taken without fear of reprisals and communication is open and straightforward. In a low trust environment, there's concern about people talking behind your back or ridicule in the case of failure.

- How does this resonate for you?

Dynamism and Liveliness

A highly dynamic situation is when new things occur often and alternative ways of thinking and handling issues often occur. The atmosphere is lively, full of positive energy and action.

- Do you gain energy from your work and does the day move quickly, as opposed to low energy and a slow drudgery day?

Playfulness

A relaxed atmosphere is one with good-natured joking and humour that can help people relax.

- Is the environment one where it's okay to be playful, or is it highly restricted?

Debate

In debating organisations, many voices are heard and people are keen to put their ideas forward. Where debates are missing, people follow authoritarian patterns without questioning.

- Does debate focus on the issue and are different perspectives accepted?
- Is new thought accepted within an environment of mutual respect that can provide greater insight?

Conflict

When a level of conflict is high, groups and individuals dislike each other and the climate can be characterised as warfare. There's personal tension, so in debating an issue it becomes less about the idea and more personal.

- Do you and staff withdraw or operate in any degree of fear within the workplace?

Risk-Taking

In the high risk-taking climate, bold new initiatives can be taken even when the outcomes are unknown. People feel as though they can take a gamble and are willing to risk putting ideas forward.

- How is uncertainty dealt with in the environment?
- Are people concerned about trying something new or are they more concerned about making a mistake?
- Is this an environment that supports risk-taking, where it's okay to experiment and failure is seen as a potential learning opportunity?

Idea Time

In the high idea time, the possibilities exist to discuss and test fresh suggestions. Creativity is enriched with time to reflect.

- Are you encouraged to think, experiment and look for alternatives to challenges that arise?

Tally up your responses to assess your thoughts about the workplace approach. Undertaking this exercise helps you determine whether you're being enabled to be creative and, as a manager, whether you're providing the conditions for the team to be safe in creativity.

Are you in an environment where failure is not just tolerated but celebrated, or an atmosphere where ideas are debated to ensure the best idea can be progressed, or where missed deadlines don't seize people with fear? If not then it's unlikely you're in an environment that will enable you to be highly motivated and be your best creative self.

Reflection – Part 2
What do you consider important to support your intrinsic motivation?

So given motivation is such an important factor in workplace creativity, let's next reflect on what are the intrinsic motivators you could need to be at your creative best.[95]

Apply the following to your current role and consider how this awareness might change the way you think about your motivation.

Consider the following:

Does your role provide an intellectual challenge?

Research that seeks input from workers through interviews and surveys consistently points to a large proportion of people being motivated by the intellectual challenge of the role. This is particularly the case with roles with a research component.

Challenge is defined as the 'perception that jobs and or tasks are challenging, complex and interesting – yet at the same time not overtaxing or underwhelming'. This links back to the concept of flow and being in a state where you're absorbed in the task. Finding roles that challenge you will help increase your time in flow. But this relies on having the skills to rise to the challenge, otherwise, it will result in increased anxiety.[96]

How much independence or autonomy do you need in your role?

Researchers have found that creativity is dramatically enhanced when employees are given the freedom to decide how they do their jobs. Managers have an important role to play here to ensure they define clear goals to ensure staff know what they're aiming for and don't shift the goalposts along the way.[97]

Research also shows that when jobs are complex and demanding, that is they're high on challenge, autonomy and complexity, the employees are more likely to focus their attention and effort. This makes them more persistent and more likely to consider different alternatives, which should result in creative outcomes.[98]

Does the role enable pursuing your passions?

Some people are simply more revolutionary in their thinking than others and are suited to more radical projects. These people need to be well matched to a project, giving them licence to be independent. They should, in some part, set their own agendas through spending a percentage of their time on projects of their own choosing. It's particularly important with creative and innovative projects that these are matched with people with the appropriate set of skills and have the resources that enable them to rise to the challenge.[99]

What type of management engagement do you appreciate?

Managers can still make a difference and a good leader can inspire creative work. A manager's engagement and attitude to a project can be the defining factor in individual and team creative responses. This points to a manager's role as an 'appreciate audience'. It also reinforces that seemingly little things like public recognition can go a long way in maintaining motivation.[100]

Are you averse or embracing of failure?

This catch cry of embracing failure is relevant for both managers and individuals. There's more acceptance in management that they should aim to create environments that decrease the fear associated with failure and reframe this as experimentation and learning. This is easier said than done as the fear of failure can rise with the scale of the business. As managers and workers, can the history of failure be reframed to improve your creative problem-solving, team learning and organisational performance?[101]

Assessing an organisation for creativity

The previous questions asked you to reflect on what you seek in a role, what motivates you and to be clear about this, rather than leave this to chance.

The third reflection provides you further prompts when seeking a new role, either as areas to research about the organisation, or as possible questions to ask your prospective employer to be sure it's the right fit for you. In building a picture about the organisation, you'll get a better sense of the daily work environment and some of the micro processes at play that influence both the staff and the organisation's approach or tolerance for creativity.

Reflection - Part 3
What should I look for in a future employer?[102]

Let's start with organisational structure:
- Does the organisation still think of creativity as sitting with a few creative types, (do they still believe in the lone inventor myth) or do they recognise that creative breakthroughs are drawn from many contributions?
- Test this by noting or asking how this shows up in the structure and the networking within the organisation. Are ideas generated from a centralised and top-down process or tapped into (possibly by technology platforms) that staff feed into? To what degree is time for networking encouraged?
- How hierarchical is the organisation? Flatter structures in small- to medium-sized organisations can assist with creative outputs by enabling more people to speak up.
- How bureaucratic is the organisation or how many layers of management are you working within?
- Creativity feeds on vibrant ongoing collaborations and free idea flow but this can be challenging to maintain as organisations, business units and projects become too large. In this case, seek information on how technology is used to support collaboration.

Embracing diverse perspectives:
- How diverse is the organisation? This could show up as staff from different disciplines, ethnic backgrounds, areas of expertise and social identities, all data that should be available in their annual report. The research shows that creative work is more likely to combine in exciting ways in workplaces with diverse skills and thinking styles, and with mechanisms to share these views.
- Does the organisation encourage views from outside the organisation whether in person, through networks or open source innovation?

Project management:
- Not every idea is worth pursuing, so how are ideas culled and through what process?

- How are projects managed through the bureaucracy? Is there a clear pathway to ensure creative ideas or projects are protected with checkpoints through to decision-making?

Information sharing:

- How are ideas shared, problems discussed and collaborative teams created? How do managers involve others in thinking together in innovative ways?
- Research points to the need for both a structured approach to information technology and a broad fostering of communication throughout the culture. Even when staff know each other and work relatively near each other, it can still be difficult to bring ideas and expertise together at the right time and in the right way to spark a creative act.[103]
- Can staff who don't normally interact exchange ideas? Do they have informal, light-touch networks to enable unanticipated exchanges of information?

In summary, by asking and researching these questions, you can determine how this additional information could influence the way you think about this organisation.

CHAPTER 9

Managing Creativity Versus Managing For Creativity

What role does management play in fostering the creative process in the workplace?

When it comes to the success of creative projects, management and supervision rate highly in the research. Professor Amabile refers to the 'power of ordinary practices', suggesting managers should pay attention to the details of their own everyday and seemingly mundane behaviours with their staff.[104]

It's in the context of culture, that managers can take note of the accumulation of small, everyday thoughts and habits that generate and sustain culture.[105] Managers can support their staff and get the best from teams by performing both task-oriented behaviours (activities that provide clarity, resources and structure to staff) and relationship-oriented behaviours (including being supportive, empathic and considerate of their feelings).[106]

The clear links between work environment and creativity neatly fall into six general categories. For managers these provide clear practical areas of focus when aiming to enhance creativity in the workplace. The six areas are challenge, freedom, resources, work-group features, supervisory encouragement and organisational support.[107]

Reflection – Are you managing for creativity?

If you're a manager, try this self-evaluation exercise and assess to what degree you're managing for creativity and, if not, where you might focus to develop your own, and staff, creative competencies.

Challenge:

The research suggests that of all areas a manager can focus on to stimulate creativity, the most effective is to match people with the right role to enable them to make the best use of their expertise, creative skills and intrinsic motivation. As we learnt with flow, we're looking to engage staff in activities that have a balance between the difficulty of the task and the right degree of challenge with a person's abilities. The amount of stretch is important as too easy leaves a person bored and too hard leaves them frustrated and threatened by loss of control. Managers can also fall into the trap of giving jobs to whoever is available at the time due to the urgency of the task.[108]

As a manager ask yourself:

- Do I set tasks based on a detailed assessment of staff with the requirements of the project?

Freedom:

We know that autonomy figures highly in staff satisfaction, so ensuring the goals are clear and remain as stable as possible gives people freedom in how they approach their work. This will feed both intrinsic motivation as well as a sense of ownership. But be careful if the team has not been given a lot of freedom in the past, as people need to experience autonomy and gain confidence before they start to show a significant increase in their creativity.[109]

As a manager ask yourself:

- When I allocate tasks to my staff, am I doing this in name only by supposedly 'empowering' staff, but falling short by granting autonomy in name only?
- When organisational priorities change, am I communicating this to staff to bring them along with me?

Resources:[110]

The two main resources managers have are time and money, so deciding how much of each to give staff, a team or the project is an important call. Some organisations still use fake deadlines or impossibly tight ones to spur creativity. Although time pressures may drive people to work, it more commonly doesn't enable them to think creatively.

While research shows when staff are under time pressure it can still yield some creativity, tight deadlines didn't enable collaboration and can lead people to feel they're on a treadmill. Low time pressure doesn't necessarily foster creative thinking either, but it can if people can do so when encouraged to learn, play with ideas and develop something truly new.

The trick is to use unavoidable constraints to help build a better end product by using the boundaries to help find a solution. Constraints can provide a starting point to the problem to be solved, aiding our ability to generate and shape novel ideas. The most creative people and organisations embrace constraints and focus their attention on coming up with solutions that work inside a set of limitations: 'A lack of resources may not be the true constraint, just a lack of resourcefulness'.[111]

Where time pressure can't be avoided, managers should focus on protecting staff from interruptions, distractions and unrelated demands. The pressure can be softened by getting into the mindset of being on a mission, sharing a sense that the work is vital and the urgency is legitimate.

Driving innovative cultures also means allocating resources to unstructured staff time enabling them to work on passion projects or incubate ideas of benefit to the organisation. These initiatives work best when staff are also supported with skills to innovate and training in topics like design and agile thinking.[112] These organisations also allocate staff with coaching roles to facilitate staff progress towards their goals and delivery of the business outcomes.[113]

As a manager ask yourself:

- When staff are under time pressure, have I sufficiently explained why the time frame is necessary? Have I ensured it's not an arbitrary deadline?
- Is there scope to drive innovation by allocating time and funds for staff exploration?
- Am I ignoring work overload leading to fatigue? Staff experiencing fatigue can be more rigid in their thinking and take longer to reason correctly.[114] Remember we may imagine we can multitask, but the brain is not built to do so.

Work Group Features:

Building teams that come up with creative ideas means paying attention to the design of those teams. We know that mutually supportive and diverse teams can combine in exciting ways, where ideas emerge ideally in constructive conflict that comes with divergent minds. While recognising that managers can find this uneasy, truly creative conflict requires a diverse array of personalities, backgrounds, thinking styles and attitudes.[115]

The trap is putting together a homogenous team that may work well but is at the risk of agreeing on solutions too quickly. This acts as an echo chamber, where the team is not challenging each other and not using their expertise and creative skills to get to an innovative result. Author David Burkus refers to the 'cohesive myth', popularised by images of open-plan offices, relaxed dress codes, free food, pool tables and filled with smiling people. The myth is based on the notion that creative ideas come from teams that can suspend all criticism to focus just on cohesion. The focus on getting along all the time can come with self-censoring and reducing the ability to critique.

This has been confused with the value gained from debate, challenge and structured conflict.

The research confirms that testing and strengthening the value of ideas comes with 'conflict, evaluation, and confrontation bought about by expressing and debating differing viewpoints and drive teams to an overall more creative output'.[116]

Research also shows that teams that demonstrate job-relevant diversity are typically cross-functional and have a good spread of different educational backgrounds and expertise.[117]

Consider also the preferences staff display in working together, what's known as cognitive differences. These are the varying approaches to perceiving and assimilating data, making decisions, solving problems and relating to others. They can reveal themselves in our work styles and decision-making activities.[118]

Play is one way to create positive interactions between team members. This doesn't mean wasting time on frivolous activities, but instead creating a playful environment where experimentation and levity are encouraged. The approach is supported by neuroscience research that demonstrates that staff are more likely to solve complex problems when they're in a positive mood.[119]

As a manager ask yourself:

- Do I know the individuals well enough to put together the best team for the required task?
- Do the staff share excitement over the team's goal? Do they display a willingness to help each other during difficult periods? Do they recognise the unique knowledge and perspective that they each bring?
- Do I walk the talk and encourage being challenged or do I engage in negative debate?
- Am I providing feedback to the whole team and individuals to strengthen team buy-in on the outcome?
- What's the organisation's recruitment approach, does it hire people for diversity or homogeneity?

Supervisory Encouragement:[120]

The research clearly shows the connection between encouragement and intrinsic motivation, particularly in sustaining creativity. This means being alert to the motivational rewards at play, both intrinsic and extrinsic, acknowledging innovative efforts, meeting new ideas with an open mind and responding to them in a timely manner. Given that not every idea is worth pursuing, it also means transparent organisational and management approaches to accepting or culling ideas.

Managers can also serve as role models, persevering through tough problems, displaying creative problem-finding and solving techniques, as well as encouraging communication and collaboration.

Consider also the nature of how feedback is given: frequent versus infrequent. Infrequent feedback refers to annual performance reviews usually linked to a salary and/or bonus. Research now suggests that infrequent feedback can lead to greater stress for employees and diminishes creativity. Staff will do what is safe, what they know will work and avoid taking risks for fear of a negative review. The research notes that by providing more regular feedback employees have an opportunity to modify behaviours before deep-seated patterns and expectations are set. It makes sense that if you want staff to be creative, you need to design an environment where incentives are aligned to goals.[121]

As a manager ask yourself:

- Do I have an unconscious negative bias that means I look for reasons why an idea may not work instead of reasons to explore it further? How am I responding to team members who tend to react critically to new ideas?
- Am I primarily focused on extrinsic motivation as a means to reward staff, missing the opportunity to fuel staff's intrinsic motivation?
- Knowing what doesn't work can be just as useful as knowing what does work. How do I manage staff whose ideas don't pan out?
- How do I give feedback? Do I enable the idea to be developed, finding solutions to small problems on the way to tackling a larger, looming challenge? Is the feedback timely?
- How do I demonstrate my support to staff? Consider supportive behaviours like genuinely demonstrating emotional support, keeping in regular contact, recognising positive outcomes privately and publicly and consulting staff by seeking their advice and respecting ideas.
- Have I created an environment where staff expect to receive constructive developmental feedback on their work? Am I helping staff define the problems that are worth pursuing?
- Managers need to stress information giving and sharing of constructive feedback to foster employee creativity. Is creativity positively evaluated but never rewarded?[122]

Organisational Support:[123]

Consider what measures and messages are in place that encourage creativity across the organisation. Supportive organisations consistently appreciate, reward and recognise creative efforts.

They're also organisations that value information sharing and collaboration as they recognise the exchange of ideas and data build collective knowledge, expose staff to dynamic creative thinking and are overall a more playful and fun place to be.

Managers who see innovation as part of their role actively seek out different viewpoints, getting out of the office, testing prototypes, asking questions and seeking feedback through a diverse range of networks. Leaders at innovative companies spend 50 per cent more time on 'discovery activities' than their counterparts at non-innovative organisations and make connections between seemingly disparate bits of information.[124]

As a manager ask yourself:

- Am I engaging in discovery activities to seek out new ideas from a range of sources?
- How rigid is the organisational structure? Is it contributing to silo thinking?
- Have I identified champions to add value to the idea's maturity? Am I acting as a cheerleader assisting to persuade others of the idea's potential value to move it forward?
- How is failure treated and how are hurdles overcome within the entire organisation? This points to a culture that builds resilience and confidence across the organisation.

Diversity in practice

Complexity scientist Scott Page wrote in *The Difference*, that in many problem-solving contexts, diversity provided more value than expertise. He wrote, 'If you already have four brilliant statisticians working on a policy problem, even a mediocre sociologist or economist may add more value to your team than another brilliant statistician'.[125] The logic is that when dealing with complicated problems, even smart people can get stuck, so adding a new and different perspective can help bring a fresh view or skill.

The Creative Advantage has emphasised the value of diversity – of views, people and places, as a means to introduce opportunities for creativity. While it's importance can't be underestimated, it's also recognised that diversity can be challenging.

While the evidence is overwhelming that cognitive diversity within teams is more effective in the longer term, this may not be how it seems to those within the teams. Diverse teams work harder, possibly because they fear their views will be challenged by someone who is not like-minded. Homogeneous teams, while they may feel more comfortable, may become complacent. So, faced with more cohesion versus more openness, managers are tempted to go with cohesion.[126]

Author Tom Harford provides four lessons to help managers get out of their bonding comfort zones to increase a team's creative capacity.[127]

1. Recognise our tendency to spend more time with people who look and sound like us. So, look for opportunities to find people, places and situations to engage in new kinds of interactions.
2. Value people who connect together in disparate teams as they play a bridging role and are able to knit together teams to build trust.
3. Remind yourself that tension can bring benefits that, if managed, can bring about creative sparks.
4. Believe that the ultimate goal of collaboration is something worth achieving and worth the messy awkwardness that may result.

From manager to transformational leader

In the VUCA world, is it enough to just manage or is there more we can aim for, recognising the complex social, environmental and economic problems our world is faced with? These modern problems, where past experience may not be sufficient, require more novel and, yes, creative ways of approaching them.

Global competition, new production techniques and rapid technological change have placed a premium on creativity and innovation.[128] These are often high-risk, high-reward environments where managers are required to balance both competing organisational agendas with creative innovative strategies. The leadership of creative efforts can be complicated as the leader is required to shape a creative idea into a viable innovative product or service.

There's a strong case put forward by both business leaders and researchers that creativity is a core competency skill. To lead both people and an organisation requires expertise, direct and indirect influence tactics and creative problem-solving abilities.[129] Researcher Professor Michael Mumford, says a leader's performance within an organisation is based on the degree to which they can successfully facilitate others towards meaningful goals as well as the ability to circumvent and resolve issues that impede progress. Leadership performance is directly related to an individual's capacity to use their creative problem-solving skills to resolve complex social problems.[130]

Transformational leadership is clearly much more than being a spectator or leaving creativity to chance. It's a form of leadership at the highest level of development, being self-aware of areas you need to improve and mastery in the use of tools and the process of creativity.[131]

There's no doubt that effective leadership is critical to the success of organisational creative and innovative efforts. Having teams of highly creative people is of little use without the leadership to guide and mobilise them. Whether it's a management or leadership role, individuals in these positions must recognise that creativity and creativity problem-solving are twenty-first century leadership skills. The keys to making change stick are knowledge and consistency, having a strong understanding of the creative tools and techniques to facilitate progress and using the creative process whenever solving a problem.[132]

Manager's Guide to Enhance Creativity

What types of behaviours does a manager display who's interested in getting the best creative expertise from individuals, the best cohesiveness from their team and the best outcome for their organisation? Here's a guide to remind managers what's important to help enhance creativity in the workplace.[133]

Remember:

Managers are not the sole fount of ideas

- Be the appreciative audience
- Give staff autonomy
- Ask the inspiring questions
- Allow ideas to bubble up from the workforce
- Use divergent discussion to uncover imaginative alternatives and convergent discussion to select an option
- Keep the systems open

Managers enable collaboration

- Combat the lone inventor myth
- Define 'superstar' as someone who helps others to succeed
- Use collaboration, metaphors, analogies and stories to help teams conceptualise together
- Depersonalise conflict and take the sting out of intellectual disagreement
- Create an environment that makes people feel good about participating

Managers enhance diversity

- Encourage staff with different backgrounds and expertise to work together
- Encourage individuals to gain diverse experiences that will increase creativity
- Open up the organisation to outside creative contributors and cross-fertilisation of ideas

Managers map the stages of creativity and tend to their different needs

- Allocate time to the four stages of creativity* *see below*
- Avoid process management in the fuzzy front end
- Set clear goals and don't change the goalposts
- Provide sufficient time and resources for exploration

Managers accept the inevitability and utility of failure

- Create psychological safety to maximise learning from failure
- Recognise the different kinds of failure and how they can be useful
- Create good mechanisms for filtering ideas and culling dead-end projects

Managers motivate with intellectual challenge

- Protect the front end from commercial pressure
- Clear paths through the bureaucracy for creative ideas
- Let people get on with it to do 'good work'
- Show the higher purpose of projects whenever possible
- Grant as much independence as possible

*The four stages of creativity:

- *Clarify* and spend time getting a clear understanding of the challenge
- *Ideate* to generate broad concepts and possibilities without judgement
- *Develop* by analysing potential solutions, examining strengths and thinking though steps
- *Implement* to take action on ideas, giving structure so the ideas become a reality.

SECTION 4

Optimising the Creative Advantage for Well-Being

CHAPTER 10

The Significance of Everyday Creativity

> A creative style of living, coping with difficulties and weaving possibilities, can not only produce useful accomplishments for self and the world but can offer the creator new resilience, perspective, aliveness in the moment, joy and purpose in life. – Scott Barry Kaufman[134]

Let's continue to explore how creativity can assist through our life cycle with a focus on overall well-being as we mature and age. Up to now we've considered how creativity might assist us in various roles, as parents, educators, mentors, managers, leaders and employees. In these contexts, we're utilising our innate ability to problem find and solve, but what about in other contexts as a means to further our personal development in life?

Here we reintroduce everyday creativity and consider how we might shape and realise our vision for a life well lived and what role creativity can play in this.

Everyday creativity is about personal creativity and is central to our way of life. While it's expressed as little-c creativity, it doesn't exclude Big-C creativity that we might undertake like writing a novel, contributing to a large social issue or launching the next disruptive social enterprise. In many ways it's equally as important to Big-C creativity as it might lead to discoveries where we bring novel, original and relevant ideas into action.

In thinking about everyday creativity as a creative advantage, this can provide enormous potential for originality, adaptation and improvisation. In this chapter will explore how both the concept and practice of everyday creativity can assist us to thrive throughout our lifespan by:

- Identifying the intersection of well-being and creativity
- Highlighting the health benefits associated with creative art practices
- Demonstrating how both brain health and learning can be enhanced through creative practices
- Promoting creative approaches as we age.

Many things we do each day appear common and uneventful. Dr Ruth Richards, psychologist and psychiatrist, reminds us that creativity is as much about how we do it (the process) as it is about what we do (the product). She believes we can live better lives by being consciously creative when we undertake these seemingly uneventful everyday tasks.

Her research has developed a way of measuring creativity, known as the *Lifetime Creativity Scales* (LCS), which involved developing rating scales based on data about real-life creative accomplishments at work and leisure. She was interested in the originality of everyday life, ranging from the fully unique to the unusual settings they emerged in. Over many years this research displayed the creative ingenuity of the everyday, from how a single mother made clothes on a tight budget, a father modified a wheelchair for his disabled son, an amateur archaeologist made special finds on his digs, to an auto mechanic who created his own tools. It highlighted the many forms of creativity, often before it was clearly identified or named by the actual participants.[135]

While creativity needs to be novel and appropriate, Dr Richards's research focuses on maximising the underlying creative potential in each of us, whether the outcome meets an immediate need or not.[136]

Everyday creativity is not about the trivia of life. It's about things that might lead to a discovery from where a more important accomplishment can grow. In pursuing a creative life every day, we can explore new possibilities and self-expression as a way of being, and experimentation as a style of existing.[137]

It's also where we see the relevance of Abraham Maslow's self-actualisation model of creativity and the development of self, which he believed helps us to grow and develop as human beings.[138]

The Need To Be Creative

We've learnt that most creative people are intrinsically motivated, so much so that they lose track of time. When they focus on what they're doing, they forget about everyday problems and are oblivious to distractions - these are known as peak experiences.

In the 1950s psychologist Abraham Maslow began work focused on the positive life-affirming aspects of human behaviour. Up to this time, the focus had been on psychological disorders and mental illness and considered what was 'wrong' with people. Maslow's focus was on what was 'right' with people. His work on human motivation included observation of our innate curiosity.[139]

He created a framework called the *Hierarchy of Needs*, which has led to shaping modern psychology. This motivational theory originally comprised of a five-tier model depicting human needs in hierarchical levels starting with what people need to survive through to what they need to thrive.[140]

The needs lower down the hierarchy focus on our basic survival including shelter, food and sleep. This also includes the need for safety and security.

As you move up the hierarchy to higher-oriented needs, there is our need for love and belonging to a community. The psychological needs then reach further into relationships, the love for others and ourselves and the feeling of accomplishment through self-esteem.

The hierarchy is completed with self-actualisation, finding meaning and purpose in life. Maslow believed that people are not just trying to survive, but to improve, find meaning in life and to be immersed in creative activities to reach their greatest potential.

The study of peak experiences continued with another modern-day positive psychologist, Mihaly Csikszentmihalyi. His research looked at answering the question: *'What makes us happy in everyday life?'* His early focus was on artists and scientists, to understand why they undertook and found happiness in their work, many in lieu of fame or fortune. He concluded that they found meaning in their activities, through continued practice, to achieve a higher level of mastery that allowed them to enter a special state of mind. He called the complete immersion in an activity *'flow'*.

Maslow described the mental state of flow as:

> Being completely involved in an activity for its own sake. The ego falls away and time flies. Every action, movement, and thought follows inevitably from the previous one, like playing jazz. Your whole being is involved, and you're using your skills to the utmost.[141]

Csikszentmihalyi believes when people are completely involved in the process of creating, losing themselves in that activity, they're truly happy. Maslow might have described this as a 'peak experience', found at the highest level of his hierarchy model and which everyone could experience. These internal and external motivational aspects of creativity are important when we consider how we can encourage our own and other's peak experiences.

Hierarchy of Needs by Maslow[142]

Self Fulfillment Needs
- **Self actualisation**
- Achieving full potential, creative activities

Psychological Needs
- **Esteem needs:** feeling of accomplishment
- **Belonging and love needs:** intimate relationships, friends

Basic Needs
- **Safety needs:** security, safety
- **Physiological needs:** food, water, warmth, rest

The intersection of creativity and well-being

We may think intuitively that living an everyday creative life will increase our sense of well-being because it feels good. There's now growing data to show that it can be also be associated with increased happiness and mental health.

Psychologists have defined well-being as a focus on happiness and positive emotions, or a deeper focus on living life in a full and deeply satisfying way.[143] This form of well-being includes the dimensions of autonomy, mastery, purpose in life, personal growth, positive relations with others and self-acceptance.[144]

Well-being can also be defined as a sense of balance that can be affected by life events or challenges. We feel a stable well-being when we have the behaviours, skills and resources we need to meet any psychological, social and/or physical challenges that may arise.[145]

Our positive sense of well-being can be further linked to motivation and to the work of author Daniel Pink. His studies concluded that motivational behaviours depend on three of these well-being dimensions – namely a sense of autonomy, mastery and purpose. His research shows that people with intrinsic motivation display self-direction and a devotion to becoming better at something that matters to them, which connects to their larger quest for excellence and to a purpose. He goes on to say that science confirms that this behaviour is essential to being human and, now in a world of rapid change, it's also critical for personal, professional and organisational success of any kind.[146]

Neuroscience explains that this unconscious brain state relates to survival and the tendency to keep going. It ensures we don't get distracted by destructive habits or addictions that can derail us. The stronger our sense of purpose, the more reward our brain receives from not being distracted from our goal.[147]

Negative motivators can creep in when we have a lull in momentum, when it feels like we're not progressing our goals. This is the time to identify distractions, or what could be subconsciously sabotaging our positive efforts. This is another prompt to raise our awareness of time-wasting apps, or demotivating tactics that could be sidetracking us.

Finally, even happiness is linked to creativity and we look to psychologist and author Dr Martin Seligman, for his theories on positive psychology and well-being. Dr Seligman believes we can become lastingly happier by using our signature strengths more often and in new ways – strengths such as wisdom, honesty, spirituality, kindness, gratitude, curiosity, and, of course, creativity.[148]

As we weave these concepts together, we can start to plot a pathway to a creative life every day. Creativity encompasses both well-being and motivation and at their intersection, we find the essential dimensions of purpose, mastery and autonomy. We've already seen these all figure highly in enhancing creativity in the workplace. We'll also see that they have a large influence on how we can experience creativity in everyday life.

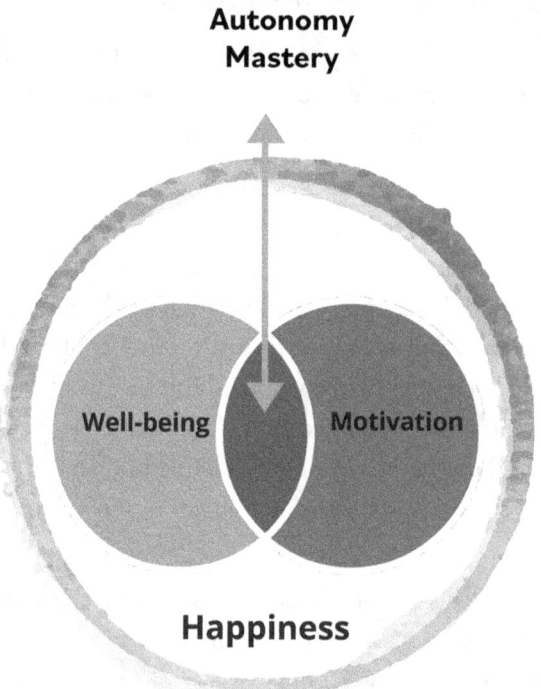

The motivational essentials

To recap, Daniel Pink defines essential purpose, mastery and autonomy as:[149]

Autonomy is acting with choice. People are at their best when they have autonomy over what they do (task), when they do it (time), who they do it with (team) and how they do it (technique).

Mastery requires engagement to become better at something that matters. It's a mindset to see our abilities as infinitely improvable and requires effort and deliberate practice.

Purpose is by nature what humans seek. Progressive organisations are building a new purpose and motive into the way they do business, with policies that enable employees to pursue purpose alongside profit. If we consider this from a more personal perspective it may be translated into our 'why', that is, why we do what we do.[150]

Reflection – Leverage your advantage to expand your everyday motivation and well-being

Okinawa in Japan is known for the long and healthy lifestyles of its centenarian residents. The Blue Zone studies have found that the Okinawans have a strong sense of what they call *'ikigai'* which literally translates to 'the reason I get up in the morning'.[151]

Creativity is closely linked to well-being and a sense of purpose through our intrinsic motivation and can even result in higher levels of happiness. In leading a balanced and happier life, consider how you might introduce or expand current behaviours that enhance your intrinsic motivation.[152]

Whether it be little-c creativity that you can explore in daily life or Big-C creativity through undertaking those larger acts, where can you carve out a space that enables you to have autonomy, mastery and purpose in your everyday life?

Consider how you might:

- Update your environment at home, work or school to enable your need for autonomy, whether it be over the tasks you undertake, how you spend your time, what techniques you use and what resources, stimuli or team you draw upon.
- Act on a desire to get better at something that matters, where you're so engaged, you enter into the state of flow. Hard work and dedicated practice are often a prerequisite for creativity, particularly Big-C creativity. Big-C artists, inventors, scientists, and authors spend years mastering their respective domains before making a valued creative contribution.
- Approach mastery. Flow doesn't guarantee mastery, so are you approaching this with a learning goal or a growth mindset? This is an expansive mindset that keeps you working in spite of the difficulty to find inventive strategies. It also means you care enough to put the effort into pursuing mastery in your domain.[153]
- Consider as you strive towards mastery, are you doing this in service of some greater purpose, objective and desire larger than yourself?

CHAPTER 11

Everyday Creativity Through the Arts

We know that creative approaches can lead to innovation across many domains. But what about a more 'hands-on' experience through art practices that enable us to express ourselves creatively?

There's been a growth in studies that quantify the mental health and overall well-being benefits of creative practices. Engaging in creative activities has been attributed to improving rates of depression, reducing the body's response to stress, assisting with cognitive decline, boosting the immune system to an increase in happiness.

Participating in the arts through everyday little-c creative activities and utilising the creative potential that we all possess at any age, by engaging in dancing, drawing, painting, performing and more broadly craft making, are being understood as an essential part of a holistic healthcare system.

Crafting a healthier mindset

Research is showing that hand-based craft activities have a direct and quantifiable benefit through their meditative action, activating brain areas that correspond, and even contributing to a sense of calm and an improved emotional state.[154] Yarn crafts such as knitting and crochet often incorporate mental challenges that assist to develop eye-to-hand coordination, fine motor dexterity and act to increase our attention spans. They also provide a space for mindfulness and, when undertaken in a group setting, can reinforce social connections.

For over a century, arts and crafts have been a core part of occupational therapy emerging after World War One in response to the post-traumatic stress disorders experienced by returned soldiers. Crafts like knitting and basket weaving were offered to shell-shocked soldiers both as a diversion therapy to take their minds off their pain and the associated negative thoughts, as well as skill development geared towards re-entering the civilian workforce.[155]

Fast forward to today and it's been shown that repetitive actions undertaken with crafts like knitting, crochet, needlework, woodwork and ceramics allow one to enter a flow state, the perfect immersive state of balance between skill and challenge.[156]

Research is also showing that making art can lead to a reduction of cortisol, a biological indicator used to measure conditions in the body such as stress. The higher a person's cortisol level, the more stressed a person is likely to be. Studies have shown that cortisol levels, taken before and after an art-making session, resulted in a statistically significant lowering of cortisol levels. Participants of the study provided written feedback that indicated that they found the art-making session to be relaxing, enjoyable and helpful for learning about new aspects of self.[157]

So what really is stress?

Neuroscientist Dr Sarah Mckay says that stress is a 'highly nuanced orchestrated response to a real or imagined threat or challenge that includes biological, behavioural, cognitive and emotional elements'.[158] The ability to respond to a threatening situation is critical for survival but long-term exposure to stress has detrimental effects on the body and brain. The effects of stress vary at different stages in life depending on the brain areas that are developing or the degree of stress exposure, with early childhood, adolescence and ageing the most vulnerable periods.[159] But just because you're stressed doesn't mean you're not coping as not all stress is bad. Good stress, eustress, is the type that can motivate and facilitate learning and change.

Creative health: innovative approaches to healthcare[160]

Consider a future where doctors, instead of prescribing tablet medication, advise you to take up a new creative art and craft to improve your mental and physical health. This scenario is getting closer with numerous research findings pointing to the demonstrated positive impact of the arts. In this age of medication dependency and expensive healthcare, it points to the enormous benefits of an arts-based healthcare system.

The evidence shows how arts-based approaches can help people stay well, recover faster, manage their long-term health conditions and experience a better quality of life overall. The United Kingdom is leading this discussion with healthcare and government professionals calling for informed and open-minded studies to progress this approach. There's also growing recognition that the medical professions are under increased pressure to meet their patients' needs. GPs know that people are living longer and in some cases are socially isolated with less community support.

Social prescribing' refers to situations where GPs prescribe activities in the community, in preference to prescribing medication. GPs integrate these activities into their suite of healthcare offerings, referring patients to a link worker – someone familiar with the local community who will recommend social and recreational activities including therapeutic art, craft, music and dance activities to match their interests. Its strength is as a complement to, rather than a replacement of, more traditional forms of treatment. This approach is also linking social prescribing to another sad reality of modern life – loneliness and its associated symptoms of anxiety. A shift away from over-prescribing towards a more preventative approach has enormous potential to deal with disease, as well as stress, isolation and loneliness.

The benefits of creative activities on mental health

There's a growing understanding that creativity is good for us and can make us happy, but this view has lacked the studies to measure these benefits. However, an important dynamic has emerged in the studies on mental health and well-being from participating in creative art-based practice. These are showing quantifiable benefits that can complement a biomedical view by focusing on not only the sickness or its symptoms, but on the whole person, resulting in a greater impact on healing and recovery. These are activities that can be undertaken by all of us to improve our overall quality of life and leveraged more effectively for the greater public good.

Health psychologists are also recognising how the arts might be used to assist in emotional injuries, as well as self-reflection approaches to alter behaviours and thinking patterns. Research on the connection between art, healing and public health assessed more than one hundred studies in an effort to determine the creative therapies most often employed.

Four primary therapies emerged: music engagement, visual arts therapy, movement-based creative expression and expressive writing with significant positive effects on health. The researchers were specifically interested in the intentional use of these art modalities and creative processes to foster health and well-being outcomes.

The research clearly demonstrated that art-based engagement has significant positive effects on mental health:

- Music engagement can decrease anxiety and calm neural activity
- Visual arts therapy can be a refuge from the intense emotions associated with illness
- Movement-based creative expression can relieve stress
- Expressive writing can help one to process life events and can positively impact mental health.[161]

While evidence-based research takes time to show the health impacts, there are numerous recent studies demonstrating the mental and neurological benefits of art- and craft-based activities.

Here's a selection of the progress being made.

- The emergence of a vibrant art and craft movement in Christchurch, New Zealand post the 2011 earthquake is part of a growing understanding of the value of community-focused recovery responses. Studies undertaken on the role craft can play in healing post-traumatic experience illustrated its value in processing key elements of the disaster, creating opportunities for social support, giving to others, generating learning, meaning-making and developing a vision for the future.[162]
- There's been a spotlight on the role of knitting and the significant psychological and social benefits that accrue from collective participation. A major 2013 United Kingdom study from Cardiff University reported 'in a survey of 3,545 knitters worldwide, respondents who knitted for relaxation, stress relief and creativity also reported higher cognitive functioning, improved social contact and communication with others'.[163] It reported they derived a sense of accomplishment, connection to tradition, increased happiness, reduced anxiety, enhanced confidence, as well as increased cognitive abilities (improved memory, concentration and ability to think through problems).[164]
- Another study observed the benefits of introducing knitting into the lives of thirty-eight female hospital patients admitted with anorexia nervosa. The subjects were asked to report on the effects knitting had on their psychological state. The study showed 74 per cent reported feeling 'distracted' or 'distanced' from negative emotional and cognitive states, as well as more relaxed and comfortable. Over half said they felt less stressed, a feeling of accomplishment, and less likely to act on their 'ruminating thoughts'.[165] This preliminary data suggests that knitting may benefit inpatients with eating disorders by reducing their anxious preoccupations about eating, weight loss and shape control.[166]
- *Knit for Peace* in the United Kingdom carried out both a widespread literature review looking at the health benefits of this craft as well as a survey of over one thousand knitters in their network. Their report points to the effectiveness of knitting (and crochet) in helping older people become more resilient, specifically with results including improvements in mental and physical health, lowering blood pressure, distracting from pain, slowing the onset of dementia, overcoming isolation and loneliness and increasing a sense of well-being.
- This unique network also donates their finished pieces to those in need in hospitals, women's refuges, refugee drop-in centres and camps. This giving act contributes to an increased sense of usefulness, self-worth and inclusion in society, all assisting to decrease elderly knitters physical decline. Knitting can no longer be dismissed as an old-fashioned pastime as it has proven that its health-giving qualities should be seriously promoted.[167]
- Parkinson's disease (PD) is a devastating neurodegenerative disorder affecting an estimated ten million people worldwide. It causes a host of movement-related symptoms, and patients often describe challenges with

everyday tasks that require fine motor control. As their mobility decreases, patients lose their autonomy and self-confidence and suffer cognitive and mood problems. Enter 'Dance for PD', a program underpinned by peer-reviewed studies. It's designed to combat both physical and mental sides of the disorder through creativity, social interaction, and intentional movement, cued by music to activate specific brain regions. Early research shows improvements in motor and cognitive function as well as mood.[168]

- Numerous studies of community spaces and, in particular, men's sheds in Australia, are observing how these spaces are contributing to the lowering of depression in older men. Men's sheds enable older men to socialise as they participate in a range of woodwork and other activities. Studies point to a decrease of self-reported symptoms of depression and concluded the social environment, with its sense of purpose, relationships created and enjoyment, as well as learning new creative skills, could be the main contributing factor.[169] Men's sheds also have an important role to play in addressing gendered health disparity as the social focus contributes to health-related literacy.[170]

A further research consideration from these types of studies is that the benefits being evidenced could be from the social connections that art and craft gatherings enable. For those who are ill or may suffer from social anxiety or are just shy, the strength of these activities is in the coming together, enabling individuals to participate collectively. Either way it's recognised that to distract from an uncomfortable or stressful focus is in itself a valuable outcome.

The evidence is growing that a variety of arts-based approaches can improve quality of life and the associated benefits of improved mobility, mental health, speech, memory, pain, learning and more. Taking up an art-based practice, whether it be as a regular activity with the added social connections or through a more focused and deliberate practice, could potentially lower the cost and burden of chronic disease, neurological disorders and mental health issues for millions of people. The more we understand the relationship between creative expression and our physical and mental well-being, the more we'll discover the healing power of the arts.

Utilising the arts to assist learning

Evidence suggests that experience in the arts may facilitate creative thinking and effective problem-solving across a broad range of domains. These are the findings of the American National Science Foundation, which has evaluated the effects of learning from activities including musical performance, drawing, visual aesthetics and dance.[171]

They've found training in an art-based discipline shares neural networks with other higher cognitive functions. This enhances the learning effects, strengthens the brain's attention system, which in turn can improve cognition more generally.

The brain neural pathways dedicated to attention play a crucial role in learning and memory, contributing to its importance in cognitive performance. A focus on learning and performing an art discipline is shaping the brain networks through 'activity-dependent plasticity'. What we do daily is reflected in the wiring patterns of our brain and the efficiency of our brain's networks. If we find an art practice that excites our passion and engages us wholeheartedly, and we stick with it, we should notice improvements in other cognitive areas in which attention is important.[172]

Specifically, the cumulative research shows that:

- Experience with musical structure can enhance the learning of language structure. Moreover, long-term musical experience is known to last for years and it's possible that such experience may provide protective effects against brain ageing and even the disruptive effects of hearing loss.[173]
- Dance integrates the rhythm of music and the representation of language. As music and dance evoke emotions and stimulate visual imagery, they can also maintain attention, allowing a higher level of memory retention.
- Visual art learning relies on a system of perception, cognitive and motor functions, that enable a more effective network of cognitive processing.

Both art learning and production involve a complex interplay between multiple sensory, motor and higher cognitive mechanisms. The studies conclude that art should be regarded as a cognitive process and understanding how we use symbolic form to organise our thinking processes can have implications for learning.

Reflection – Where can you introduce art and craft into your well-being approach?

The goal is to find activities that light up your brain's reward centres through cognitive effort and concentration, as well as activities you're interested in and so will give you pleasure. Working with your hands becomes the catalyst, releasing serotonin and endorphins that can reduce the levels of cortisol.

Do the arts have a superpower?

A study from the Mayo Clinic sought to pinpoint various activities that either predicted cognitive impairment or protected against it during the final years of life. We know that an active social life in both midlife and late life is linked to fewer instances of mild cognitive impairment. This study also found that the creative behaviour that had the greatest protective effect, was artistic activity, such as painting, drawing, and sculpting.[174] It also observed that regularly engaging in craft activities such as woodworking, quilting or sewing was also linked to fewer incidents of mild cognitive impairment. The study supports the idea that engaging the mind creatively may protect neurons from dying, stimulate the growth of new neurons, develop new neural pathways or may help recruit new neurons to maintain cognitive activities in old age. It also found greater results when the activity began in midlife and persisted through to later life.[175]

Despite the view that the creation of art is a basic human need, playing an essential role in our evolution and ability to adapt, it's only recently that research has finally caught up to the notion that it's also something we can't afford to live without. This research is making it clear that experiencing or creating art has a dynamic effect on our brain. This form of creativity can potentially address some of the most difficult issues of our time including chronic stress and associated illnesses, pain management and addiction, learning differences, depression and mental illness, and reduced productivity and innovation. That sounds like a superpower to me!

CHAPTER 12

Maximising Our Creativity As We Age

> 'Even as we age, novelty propels ongoing plasticity ... A lifetime of creativity helps to maintain this flexibility.'[176] – Brandt and Eagleman

In the face of expected declines as we age in speed, short-term memory and deductive reasoning, how might we stay creative?[177] So far, we've focused on the benefits of thinking about little-c creativity, the types of activities that enable us to express our creative thinking abilities through everyday actions.

We've also noted that benefits can accrue when we undertake art-based practices throughout life and continue these into our mature ageing years. These activities work because they help build cognitive reserve. This refers to the brain's ability to operate effectively even when some function is disrupted. It also refers to the amount of damage the brain can sustain during ageing, before changes in cognition become evident.[178]

We can build a cognitive reserve through taking up activities that present mental or intellectual challenges. Cognitive activity is measured by the years of education or how mentally stimulating a person's job is. It's strongly associated with reduced incidences of age-related health decline. People who stay mentally active post-retirement, and for every extra year of education, have shown an 11 per cent decrease in the risk of developing dementia.[179]

Taking up mental challenges like knitting and crafts, writing, reading and discussion through book clubs, as well as physical activities combined with maintaining social connections and keeping an open mindset, are proven ways to stay cognitively alert as we age.

The good news is mental decline is not inevitable, with further evidence that some abilities can remain stable or even improve as we age. Research studies by psychologist Martin Seligman identified the cognitive factors maintained into older age including long-term memory retrieval, verbal and academic knowledge, reading ability, oral expression and listening comprehension. By preserving domain expertise and knowledge, these have been shown to compensate for overall mental decline, thus increasing the chances that creative ideas will emerge.[180] Dr Seligman notes that as we age, we start to use shortcuts involving a degree of flexibility, useful to figuring out creative solutions. Our pattern recognition is enhanced when we're faced with a novel problem because we use our memories of similar situations to resolve it.

The older we get, the more information and experiences are available to us, and the more examples of successful patterns, heuristics and intuitions we have to draw on. Seligman also emphasises that the abilities likely to improve with age may also be teachable. Teaching them explicitly should make for a more creative world.[181]

According to neuroscientist Dr Daniel Levitin, our personality traits, such as curiosity and openness to new experience, provide both a neuroprotective benefit and correlate highly with good health and long life. People who are curious are more likely to challenge themselves both intellectually and socially, enabling them to stay mentally agile.[182] He points to learning new things as one of the best ways to keep our brain active and healthy, as it ensures we continue to build new neural connections as we get older.[183]

These are the basis for the creative advantage as we age. For those who require some motivation to stay curious, we point to psychologist Carol Dweck's work on fixed and growth mindset. As with most things, these two mindsets refer to the ends of a continuum and we're rarely entirely at one end in all aspects of life. People with a fixed mindset generally have an external locus of control and are low in curiosity and openness. This may show up as not being really interested in learning new things or able to see the benefits as worth the effort. Whereas those with a growth mindset believe they can change, learn a new skill and are energised by learning. They have an internal locus of control and believe effort is sometimes its own reward and can have big payoffs.[184]

Can we change our mindset? People who actively engage in a growth mindset can, as Dr Levitin writes:

> To them, life is a journey of gathering new information, meeting new people, seeking helpful feedback from mentors or teachers and learning new skills. People of all ages with a growth mindset outperform students with a fixed mindset … you can change your brain and you can overcome limitations you've encountered previously, not just with effort, but with focussed, directed leaning … having a repertoire of approaches and perspective to draw on enriches your mental life and can spur that much-needed motivation.[185]

Brain plasticity research has shown how connectivity between neurons can change with experience, confirming the brain is malleable. These neuroscientific discoveries show us that we can increase our neural growth by the actions we take: staying curious and open and by exploring our intrinsic motivation. With deliberate practice, neural networks can grow new connections, strengthen existing ones, and build insulation that speeds transmission of impulses. This can also be enhanced by following good habits in our nutrition, movement or exercise and sleep routine.

Creativity can also be enhanced by continuing to interact with the world. The interactions don't need to be especially complex or risky. Dr Levitan points to studies where older adults were encouraged to walk around an outdoor landscape freely compared to those made to walk around a rectangular path. They showed significantly higher scores in a series of creativity tests, including divergent thinking and problem-solving tasks.[186]

The changing brain

Neurologists and psychologists are coming to the conclusion that the brain at midlife, the period defined as between thirty-five to sixty-five years of age, is more elastic and supple than previously believed. While some abilities like memory are declining, our temperament is also changing, but for the better.

Neurologist George Bartzokis says that while we may not have the same amount of information as when we were younger, in midlife we use the information better. Both the wiring and the different regions of the brain pull together to make the whole organ work better than the sum of its parts:[187]

> For all its plasticity the brain is a specialised machine, with specific regions handling specific operations. The greatest divergence comes between the left and right hemispheres ... as we age, the walls between the hemispheres seem to fall, with the two halves increasingly working in tandem.[188]

Studies on a group of adults aged between sixty-five to ninety-five years old who tested high on memory, were also tested further on a series of language, perception and motion function tasks. Results found that, compared to younger adults, high functioning older adults were using either a different hemisphere or both hemispheres at the same time.

While the brain is not programmed to get stronger as we age, the results may be showing a way that the brain compensates for the ageing decline, sometimes integrating the hemispheres efficiently resulting in better thought and reasoning processes. As the brain's flexibility improves, so too may our temperament, resulting in an increased tolerance for ambiguity and improved ability to manage relationships.[189] So, the key is to keep the brain active through introducing challenging and creative activities.

Sustaining creativity as we mature

There are clearly benefits to maintaining our brain and cognitive health regardless of the potential to influence our creative abilities. We also know that while some people creatively peak early, many will peak later in life – so can we influence this?

Professor David Galenson, an economics art historian, puts forward a social science method to describe individual creativity. Galenson believes there are two different trajectories, either *conceptual* or *experimental*, that innovators can take.[190]

Conceptual innovators do their best work early in their life, they work quickly with specific ideas they want to communicate and they articulate those ideas clearly. They plan precisely and then execute. Someone like Picasso, who burst on to the art scene, epitomises the conceptual innovator. Galenson points out Picasso's abrupt stylistic changes, tendency to plan his work in advance with great detail, and hints that his work carried a deliberate message. He would also categorise Albert Einstein as a great conceptual innovator as he made discoveries through highly abstract reasoning, with his greatest contributions early in his career.[191]

In contrast, **experimental innovators** don't display a clearly articulated idea and they don't work quickly. They don't really know where they're going when they start, and they work by trial and error producing drafts and taking time to figure out what they want to say. Galenson recognised this in the artist Cezanne, who comes back to the same subject with no clear linear plan, producing many versions until he stumbles on to the idea that seizes his imagination.[192] He would also categorise Charles Darwin as a great experimental innovator, as he spent decades accumulating evidence on evolution and its mechanisms, and made his greatest contributions later in his career.[193] Galenson writes:

> Experimental artists develop their contributions gradually and late works in their mature signature styles are typically the important examples of experimental artists' innovations, but conceptual artists often arrive at their contributions precipitously, and therefore it is generally the earliest works in a new style that are the most important.[194]

Professor Galenson's calls conceptual innovators 'sprinters' and his studies on economists who have won the Nobel Prize shows, on average, they did most of their influential work at age forty-three. Whereas the experimental innovators, the 'marathoners', did theirs at age sixty-one. Similarly, his analysis of famous poets found conceptual innovators authored their best works at twenty-eight, compared to thirty-nine for experimental innovators.[195]

In an independent study of every physicist who has ever won the Nobel Prize, exactly half were conceptual innovators working on theoretical work under the age of thirty. Among the older group of forty-five years plus, 92 per cent were undertaking experimental work.[196]

The fundamental differences between conceptual and experimental innovators become apparent when we think about the creative work they are undertaking. Conceptual innovation can be done quickly because it does not require years of methodical investigation and it's easier to come up with an original insight when approached with a fresh perspective.[197]

Galenson found that 'conceptual innovators normally make their most important contributions to a discipline not long after their first exposure to it'.[198] The challenge is to ensure we don't become entrenched in a specific way of approaching the problem or just copying original ideas due to fixed thought habits that develop due to this early success.

Conversely, while experimental innovators can take years or decades to accumulate the knowledge and skills, it becomes a more sustainable source of originality. Instead of reproducing past ideas, their experiments enable them to continue to discover new ideas.[199]

Reflection – Are you a sprinter or marathoner?

Influencing creativity as we age could be as simple as adopting an experimental approach and having the patience to run the marathon. The more experiments you attempt, the less constrained you are by ideas from the past. With trial and error, testing out different ideas to explore options, you may eventually find a new, novel and useful creative solution.

As our knowledge increases and we have more experiences, shortcuts and information to draw on, we can acquire a reflective perspective on life. Like creativity, wisdom is only found in the human species and while both change through the ageing process, they might also converge in later life. The trick is to ensure we remain cognitively active through undertaking creative thinking practices as we gracefully age.

Do you recognise these great creators?

While this is not an exact science, Dr Martin Seligman goes further and notes that creative achievement tends to peak early (in the early thirties) and drop off rapidly in domains like lyrical poetry, pure mathematics, and theoretical physics, which tend to rely heavily on fluid reasoning.

In contrast, creative achievement peaks later (in the early forties) and exhibits a more gradual decline (if any) in fields that draw more on knowledge and expertise, such as novel writing, history, philosophy and medicine. Psychologists, interestingly, fall in the middle of these two patterns, peaking around age forty.[200]

Who do you think were conceptual or experimental innovators?[201]

Consider the following great creatives and when they released their most novel, valuable or influential works: film-makers Orson Wells and Alfred Hitchcock, poets E.E Cummings and Robert Frost, scientists Albert Einstein and Watson and Crick, the writer Mark Twain and the painter Leonardo da Vinci. Were they conceptual or experimental innovators?

Creativity is our greatest asset

> To realise our true creative potential – in our organisations, in our schools and in our communities – we need to think differently about ourselves and to act differently towards each other. We must learn to be creative.
> – Sir Ken Robinson[202]

You may have had some common misconceptions about creativity when you commenced reading this book. Maybe you'd bought into the many myths that still circulate about creativity, preferring to imagine the lone creator, working alone throughout the night to come up with the eureka moment that would save us all. Or the genius artist, misunderstood and probably mad, working relentlessly on the canvas or musical score to create a masterpiece.

But really, these myths have outlived their usefulness. For one, the lone creator attributing breakthrough inventions and creative works to a sole person, ignores other influences, collaborations and the creative teams behind these breakthroughs.[203]

Or maybe you thought creativity is solely in the domain of the artistic Big-C creatives and weren't aware of the myriad of ways you may be expressing your creativity through the originality of everyday life.

Whatever you may have thought, I hope that by reframing creativity as a process of creative thinking, problem finding and problem-solving you've had an opportunity to examine where you might reconsider creativity at any stage of your life.

The main misconception this book aims to challenge is that creativity is only available to the fortunate few, with young and agile brains. Let's finally dispel the notion that creativity is something you're born and is only for playful children. Or only for those of us in specific art or music professions and, the biggest myth of all, that inevitably creativity must decline with age.

The VUCA world has forced us to rethink what worked in the past as being applicable to today's challenges. As I write we're still in the midst of an international pandemic that is challenging all parts of society with the 'new normal' being coined as many times as 'unprecedented'.

Educational intuitions may still hold on to what Sir Ken Robinson referred to as tired mantras about raising traditional academic standards that were designed for other times and other purposes.[204] However, as he went on to say: 'We will not succeed in navigating the complex environment of the future by peering relentlessly into a rear view mirror'.[205] Here we can have a significant role in influencing children and young people, to encourage and develop their creative capacities and create cultures that persevere to maintain these as they continue into their senior education.

Maybe the shining light is the corporate sector, as business has recognised that their survival depends on the constant flow of new ideas for products and services. CEOs are signalling a new direction brought forward by increasing complexity that will give rise to a new generation of leaders, fresh thinking and continuous innovation throughout their organisations.[206]

Of even further encouragement is the growing research that testifies the rich sustenance that art-based practices can play in sustaining us to live active and purposeful lives full of curiosity. Neuroscience has informed and overturned theories that lead many to believe that creativity couldn't be learnt or developed and we know that we can improve our creative abilities throughout our lifetime.

Biologically we share 98 per cent of our genetic material with chimpanzees. Now while chimpanzees may express some original behaviours, they can't express these or create cultures with these thoughts.[207] Mihaly Csikszentmihalyi, the author of the concept of *flow*, says that the privilege of being human is not just because we think original ideas, but because we can judge and evaluate our thoughts and record and preserve them in a culture. What makes us different from other life forms is the result of creative thought, and the cultural and social systems that we build with them.[208]

Creativity is within the grasp of every person, workplace and community, and is a learnt skill that with the awareness of the four essential creative elements – motivation, domain expertise, creative skill sets and the social and work environment – enables us all to create new possibilities.

We end with a quote from the master of flow, Mihaly Csikszentmihalyi, who writes:

> The creative process is what makes us totally human, and can make us happy despite all of the things that can go wrong in our lives, including death and old age. It is when we are creating that our lives are most fulfilled. By understanding how the creative process works, we have a chance to learn how to improve the quality of life for everyone, and especially for our children.[209]

Appendix

Who do you think were conceptual or experimental innovators?

210	Conceptual Innovator	Experimental Innovator
Film	Orson Wells - First feature film at age 25 (*Citizen Kane*).	Alfred Hitchcock - Three most popular films at ages 59-61 (*Vertigo*, *North by Northwest*, *Psycho*).
Poetry	E.E Cummings - First influential poem at 22 and half of his best work by age 40.	Robert Frost, 92% of most reprinted poems after 40 years of age.
Science	Watson and Crick developed a model to explain the molecular structure of DNA known as the double helix. Watson was aged 25 and Crick 37 when they published.	
	Einstein and theory of special relativity - It's thought Einstein started to think about light's behaviour when he was just 16 years old.	
Writing		Mark Twain published *Adventures of Huckleberry Finn* at age 49.
Painting		Leonardo da Vinci finished the *Last Supper* in his early fifties when he then started the *Mona Lisa*.

The Essential Elements to Creativity

The Role of Mindset

When it comes to pursuing creative endeavours and the motivation to continue, the way we approach problem-solving, the unexpected pathways these challenges may take us and the perseverance to continue through these setbacks, these all point to our belief systems and the concept of mindset.

Mindsets play out in life, throughout school, sport, the workplace, education and relationships. They'll impact what we strive for, what we see as success and whether we treat failure as a mistake or a learning.[211] Carol Dweck also believes that there is a direct link between creative people and their mindset. She writes: 'In a poll of 143 creativity researchers, there was wide agreement about the number one ingredient in creative achievement. And it was exactly the kind of perseverance and resilience produced by the growth mindset'.[212]

Mindsets are also important when we consider the people we engage with: our family, work colleagues and others we interact with. Dr Dweck's research can be extended to reflect on 'personality mindsets' and personal qualities. For example, how dependable, cooperative, caring or socially skilled you or others are.[213]

Understanding Deliberate Practice

The Creative Advantage: How the intersection of science and creativity reveals life's ultimate advantage delved into the value of deliberate practice as a means to improve our domain expertise.

The work led by Professor Anders Ericsson, with contributions by over one hundred leading scientists, researched expertise and top performance in a wide variety of domains: surgery, acting, chess, writing, computer programming, ballet, music, aviation, firefighting, and many others, and led to clear conclusions.[214]

Deliberate practice requires considerable, specific, and sustained efforts to do something you can't do well – or even do at all. Research shows that it's only by working at what you can't do that you turn into the expert you want to become.[215]

Professor Ericsson defined deliberate practice as characterised by

- well-defined and specific goals
- focused and concentrated effort
- high repetition of a specific activity in a learning zone

- a coach or mentor who can share best practice approaches
- feedback to ensure the practice isn't reinforcing bad habits
- getting out of one's comfort zone.[216]

Deliberate practice works by tapping into superior reasoning methods and powers.[217] This is where the direct advantage to creative thinking can be observed, through the development of problem-solving skills, coming at problems in fundamentally different and more useful ways.

The Top Seven Skills that Make Up a Creative Skill Set

Personality and our behavioural traits can influence our approach to creativity and, in particular, the specific skills you can develop to become more creative.

The research undertaken by Drs Mandell and Jordan identifies a number of creative skills and behaviours that were consistently represented by the great masters of art. They demonstrated in *Becoming a Life Change Artist*, the 'seven creative skills'.[218] These are central to the creative success of the artist's studied, but also to the success of business leaders responsible for creating innovations in the products and services of their operations. Best of all they demonstrated that each of these skills and behaviours was able to be taught and learnt by anyone.

The seven creative skills, reflected in our behaviours, provide a highly applicable framework for anyone wishing to successfully create change in their lives, to assist them to discover how creative they really are and how much more creative they could become.[219]

Briefly, the Seven Creative Skills are:

- *Preparation* – Deliberately engaging in activities that help break us from our usual patterns of thought and feeling and prepare us for creative insight
- *Seeing* – Having the ability to discern new connections, gain fresh perspective, and stay alive to new possibilities
- *Using Context* – Understanding how the varied environments which we work and live influence our thoughts and behaviours and using that knowledge to make changes in our lives
- *Embracing Uncertainty* – Acting on the opportunities, sometimes hidden, presented by change and uncertainty
- *Risk-Taking* – Acting without certainty of outcome
- *Collaboration* – Engaging with others to help one make desired changes
- *Discipline* – Acting consistently whether or not one feels motivated.

Get More Creative Advantage

Creativity is the most fundamentally human of qualities and a unique trait of our species. This book has explored how we can use this asset to navigate the important periods in our life with both an understanding of the neuroscience and psychology behind this.

The first book in this series, *The Creative Advantage: How the intersection of science and creativity reveals life's ultimate advantage*, sought to reveal the science that's building our understanding of why some of us are more creative. What happens at the intersection of science and creativity is no longer a mystery or based on myth. Of even more relevance, creativity is a skill that can be learnt and practised, with studies showing that creativity is close to 80 per cent learnt and acquired.[220]

This book lays out the science behind creativity, to not only appreciate our creative potential but to give us all the motivation and the tools to obtain a creative advantage in all aspects of life. Through a deep dive into the science that fuels creativity, The Creative Advantage takes you through these seven key steps:

Step 1 - Clarify your Creative Strength

How do you express your creativity? Undertake the Creativity Fitness Assessment and determine what your creative strengths are, then focus on building your creative advantage.

Step 2 - Understand the Creative Fundamentals

Learn the how, what, why and when of creativity. How we define creativity, when did humans evolve to be creative, why we need to be creative and understand what's going on in the creative brain that can give you a creative advantage.

Step 3 - Explore the Essential Creative Elements

Learn how to manage the four essential elements that influence every creative outcome. They are motivation, domain expertise, creative skill sets and the social and work environment. Understanding the science behind each element provides you with a means to leverage these to your creative advantage. Then ensure you use your time effectively through the science behind deliberate practice, enhancing the seven creative skill sets and applying a mindset to build your motivation.

Step 4 - Creating the Conditions for Creativity

Learn where ideas and creativity intersect to unlock how to generate more and better ideas. Increase your brain's creative capacity to harness spontaneous insights, the power of play and be introduced to the benefits of procrastination and boredom. Then leverage visualisation to rewire your brainpower.

Step 5 – Enhance the Body – Brain Connection

Your creativity is dependent on your body and brain's health. Learn practical ways to enhance your creativity through the value of sleep, movement and restorative activities including solitude, meditation and being in nature. Then understand how the design of your physical space is crucial to your creative output.

Step 6 – Build a Creative Routine

Build your creative practice by identifying and establishing a creative routine. Learn the 'creative rhythm method' to leverage the neuroplasticity behind habit. Then overcome barriers, capture the benefits of failure and create strategies to overcome what gets in your way to ensure your creative practice sticks.

Step 7 – Learn Creative Problem-Solving Tools

Expand your creative powers. Go from ideas to action with tools that you can use for everyday and bigger problem-solving. Be transformed by applying the information learnt and make creativity a way of life.

If you have resonated with *The Creative Advantage Lifestyle*, then I encourage you to further explore how you can build this advantage into your personal and professional endeavours through a deep dive into the science that fuels creativity and this seven-step model.

This is available in book or online format, for more information go to www.thecreativecatalyst.com.au

Become a Creative Catalyst

This book is one of a three book series that includes *The Creative Advantage: How the intersection of science and creativity reveals life's ultimate advantage* and *The Creative Advantage: Activity Guide*. The series provides the foundation to how each of us can transform the way we engage in problem solving to enhance both our personal and professional lives.

I encourage you to take this interest further by tapping into the Creative Catalyst to build your creative competency, skillsets and collaborative workplace cultures. Here you'll find a range of resources, products and services to support both your individual and workplace needs. For more resources that support you to build creative capacity and problem-solving skills that result in real and positive change visit the Creative Catalyst website at www.thecreativecatalyst.com.au

References

Abraham, A. (2018) The Neuroscience of Creativity. Cambridge Uni Press, UK

Amabile, T., (2012) Componential Theory of Creativity, Working Paper, 12-096 April 26, 2012, Harvard Business School

Amabile, T., & Mueller, J., (2008) In Handbook of Organisational Creativity, Zhou, J., & Shalley, C. Lawrence Erlbaum Assoc, NY.

Bruce, M and Bridgeland, J. (2014) The Mentoring Effect: Young People's Perspectives on the Outcomes and Availability of Mentoring, Executive Summary. Retrieved from https://www.mentoring.org/resource/the-mentoring-effect/

Burkus, D. (2014). The Myths of Creativity: The Truth About How Innovative Companies and People Generate Great Ideas. Jossey-Bass US.

Carson, S. (2010). Your Creative Brain, Seven Steps to Maximize Imagination, Productivity and Innovation in Your Life. Harvard Health Publications, USA

Colvin, G. (2012). Talent is Overrated: What really separates world-class performers from everybody else. John Murray Press, UK

Doidge, N. (2007) The Brain that Changes Itself. Penguin Books, USA

Dweck, C. (2012). Mindset: How You Can Fulfil Your Potential. Little Brown Book Group, UK, 6. Pdf version

Ericsson, A and Pool, R, (2016). Peak: Secrets from the new science of expertise. Penguin Random House, UK

Feist, G. (2010) The Function of Personality in Creativity, Cambridge Handbook of Creativity, Ed Kaufman, J. & Sternberg, R. Cambridge Uni Press, UK

Galenson, D. (2009) Conceptual Revolutions in Twentieth-Century Art. Cambridge Uni Press, UK

Gelb, M. (2014) Creativity on Demand: how to ignite and sustain the fire of genius. Sounds True, USA

Gopnik, A. (2017) The Gardener and the Carpenter. Vintage Publishing, USA

Grant, A. (2016) Originals: How non-conformists change the world. Penguin Random House, UK

Harford, T. (2016) Messy: How to creative and resilient in a tidy minded world. Abacus, UK

Heffernan, M (2015) Beyond Measure: The Big Impact of Small Changes. Simon and Schuster, UK

Imber, A. (2016) The Innovation Formula. John Wiley and Sons, Australia

Kelley, T. & Kelley, D. (2013). Creative Confidence Unleashing the Creative Potential Within Us All. William Collins, UK

Levitin, D (2020) The Changing Mind: A Neuroscientist's Guide to Ageing Well, Penguin Random House, UK

Mandell, F & Jordan, K. (2010) Becoming a Life Change Artist: Seven creative skills to reinvent yourself at any stage of your life. Penguin Group, USA

Nielsen, D & Thurber, S (2016). The Secret of the Highly Creative Thinker. BIS Publishers, Netherlands

Pink, D. (2011) Drive: The Surprising Truth About What Motivates Us. Penguin, USA

Pink, D. (2005) A Whole New Mind: Moving from the information age to the conceptual age. Allen and Unwin, Australia

Puccio, G. (2014) The Creative Thinker's Toolkit. The Great Courses, The Teaching Company, USA, Transcript Book

Robinson, K. (2009) The Element: How finding your passion changes everything, Penguin USA

Robinson, K. (2011) Out of Our Minds: Learning to be Creative. Capstone Publishing, UK

Salzburg Global Seminar, The Neuroscience of Art: What are the sources of creativity and innovation? (2015) Session Report 547

Sawyer, K. (2013) Zig Zag: The surprising path to greater creativity. Jossey-Bass, USA

Seeleg, T. (2012) Ingenius: A crash course in creativity. Harper Collins, USA, 146.

Simonelli, M. Understanding Organisational Creativity in Small- to Medium-Sized Enterprises: Does Size Matter? July 2016, Research thesis, Monash University.

Swart, T. (2019) The Source: Open your mind, Change your life. Penguin Random House, UK

Suzuki, W (2016) Healthy Brain, Happy Life: A personal program to activate your brain and do everything better, Dey Street Books, USA

Time: The Science of Creativity. (2019) Time Special Edition, USA

Wagner, T. (2012). Creating Innovators: The making of young people who will change the world. Scribner, USA

Wilson, E.O. (2017) The Origins of Creativity, Penguin Random House, UK

Courses

McKay, S. The Neuroscience Academy Lecture series, Applied Science and Brain Health. http://theneuroacademy.com/

Puccio, G. Professor The Great Courses https://www.thegreatcourses.com/professors/gerard-puccio/

Free Resources

Meditation for beginners at https://zenhabits.net/meditation-guide/

Productivity resources retrieved from https://www.productiveflourishing.com/free-planners/

Podcasts

Beaty, R. Assistant Professor of Psychology at Penn State University, US, and director of the Cognitive Neuroscience of Creativity Lab, Interview 18 August 2019. Retrieved from www.abc.net.au/radionational/programs/allinthemind/creativity-and-the-a-ha-moment/11413166

Interview with Associate Professor Muireann Irish is a cognitive neuroscientist from the Brain and Mind Centre, Retrieved from https://www.abc.net.au/radionational/programs/allinthemind/dementia-sleep-and-daydreaming/11747406

Radiolab Podcast Relative Genius 29 June 2019. Retrieved from https://www.wnycstudios.org/podcasts/radiolab/articles/g-relative-genius

Websites

The Creative Catalyst http://www.thecreativecatalyst.com.au/

Edwards, B. Drawing in the Right Side of the Brain. Retrieved from https://www.drawright.com/theory

IDEO https://www.ideo.com/

Who Mentored You: Harvard Mentoring Project https://sites.sph.harvard.edu/wmy/

Endnotes

1. Sawyer, K. (2006) Explaining Creativity: the science of human innovation. Oxford University Press, USA, 14
2. Amabile, T., (2012) Componential Theory of Creativity, Working Paper, 12-096 April 26 2012, Harvard Business School, 3–4.
3. These key themes provide a neat and effective seven-step model to increase creative capacity. They also provide the foundation for a number of programs delivered through the Creative Catalyst. Check out www.thecreativecatalyst.com.au for more information.
4. Section 1 is summarised from The Creative Advantage: How the intersection of science and creativity reveals life's ultimate advantage (2021)
5. The Neuroscience of Art: What are the sources of creativity and innovation? (2015) Session Report 547, Salzburg Global Seminar, 9.
6. Wilson, E.O. (2017) The Origins of Creativity, Penguin Random House, UK,1.
7. Sawyer, K. (2013) Zig Zag: The surprising path to greater creativity. Jossey-Bass, USA, 23.
8. The difference between problem-solving and problem finding: Problem-solving uses domain-specific expertise and skills to explore an ill-defined problem to generate creative solutions. Problem finding takes a more open-ended and exploratory approach to discover novel problems that require solutions. Abraham, A. (2018) The Neuroscience of Creativity. Cambridge Uni Press, UK, 52.
9. Suzuki, W (2016) Healthy Brain, Happy Life: A personal program to activate your brain and do everything better, Dey Street Books, USA, 217. Wendy Suzuki is a Professor of Neuroscience and Psychology at the New York University Center for Neural Science and a popular science communicator.
10. Edwards, B. Drawing in the Right Side of the Brain. Retrieved from https://www.drawright.com/theory
11. Suzuki, W. (2015) Healthy Brain, Happy Life. Harper Collins, USA, 221.
12. Abraham, A. (2018) The Neuroscience of Creativity. Cambridge Uni Press, UK, 12.
    James C. Kaufman is an American psychologist known for his research on creativity. He is a Professor of Educational Psychology at the University of Connecticut in Storrs, Connecticut. Previously, he taught at California State University, San Bernardino, where he directed the Learning Research Institute.
13. Puccio, G. (2014) The Creative Thinker's Toolkit. The Great Courses, The Teaching Company, USA, Transcript Book, 32–33.
14. Colvin, G. (2012). Talent is Overrated: What really separates world-class performers from everybody else. John Murray Press, UK, 16.
15. Carson, S (2010) Your Creative Brain, Seven Steps to Maximize Imagination, Productivity and Innovation in your Life. Harvard Health Publications, USA, 60.
16. Dietrich, A. (2018) Types of Creativity, Psychonomic Bulletin and Review (2019) 26, 1–12. Retrieved from https://doi.org/10.3758/s13423-018-1517-7. Arne Dietrich is Professor of Psychology at the American University of Beirut.
17. Dietrich, A. (2018) Types of Creativity, Psychonomic Bulletin and Review (2019) 26, 3–6. Retrieved from https://doi.org/10.3758/s13423-018-1517-7
18. The Science of Creativity, (2019) Time Special Edition, USA, 12.
19. Swart, T. (2019) The Source: Open your mind, Change your life. Penguin Random House, UK, 171.
20. Feist, G. (2010) The Function of Personality in Creativity, Cambridge Handbook of Creativity, Ed Kaufman, J. & Sternberg, R. Cambridge Uni Press, UK, 117
21. Beaty, R. Assistant Professor of Psychology at Penn State University, US, and director of the Cognitive Neuroscience of Creativity Lab, Interview 18 August 2019. Retrieved from www.abc.net.au/radionational/programs/allinthemind/creativity-and-the-a-ha-moment/11413166
22. Cognitive Neuroscience of Creativity Laboratory, Penn State University. Retrieved from https://sites.google.com/view/beaty-cncl/research?authuser=0
23. Beaty, R. Assistant Professor of Psychology at Penn State University, US, and director of the Cognitive Neuroscience of Creativity Lab, Interview 18 August 2019. Retrieved from https://www.abc.net.au/radionational/programs/allinthemind/creativity-and-the-a-ha-moment/11413166

24 Doidge, N. (2007) The Brain that Changes Itself. Penguin Books, USA, preface.

25 Swart, T. (2019) The Source: Open your mind, Change your life. Penguin Random House, UK, 97.

26 Dr Michael Merzenich, neuroscientist at the University of California, quoted in HuffPost, The 10 Fundamentals of Rewiring Your Brain
Retrieved from https://www.huffpost.com/entry/the-10-fundamentals-of-re_b_9625926

27 Grey matter is greyish nerve tissue of the central nervous system mainly composed of nerve cell bodies and dendrites. Further research suggests that although cabbies displayed better memory for London-based information, they showed poorer learning and memory on other memory tasks involving visual information. This suggests that structural brain differences may have been acquired through the experience of navigating and to accommodate the internal presentation of London. Wellcome Trust Centre for Neuroimaging at University College Professor Eleanor Maguire. From Lewis, C. (2016) Too Fast To Think. Kogan Page Ltd UK, 91.

28 Amabile, T., (2012) Componential Theory of Creativity, Working Paper, 12-096 April 26, 2012, Harvard Business School, 3–4.

29 Amabile, T., (2012) Componential Theory of Creativity, Working Paper, 12-096 April 26, 2012, Harvard Business School, 3–4.

30 Deliberate Practice refers to the way you undertake getting better at something. It's specific and requires sustained effort. It is characterised by a number of features – see appendix for more.

31 While this is a brief introduction to the model, a further condensed summary is in the appendix and a more detailed outline of the key aspects is available in 'The Creative Advantage: How the intersection of science and creativity reveals life's ultimate advantage'.

32 Modified from Amabile, T., & Mueller, J., (2008). Studying Creativity, It's Processes and Its Antecedents. Chapter 2, In Handbook of Organisational Creativity, Zhou, J., & Shalley, C. (2008) 33–63, Lawrence Erlbaum Assoc, NY.

33 Creativity: How to raise a creative thinker. April 2012 About Kids Health Retrieved from https://www.aboutkidshealth.ca/Article?contentid=627&language=English

34 The Science of Creativity, (2019) Time Special Edition, USA, 89;
Markov, S. Ellis Paul Torrance-Father of modern creativity. June 2017, Genvive.
Retrieved from https://geniusrevive.com/en/ellis-paul-torrance-father-of-modern-creativity/

35 The Science of Creativity, (2019) Time Special Edition, USA, 90.

36 Mejia, Z. Billionaire Elon Musk says he was raised by books. Make it. November 2017. Retrieved from https://www.cnbc.com/2017/11/16/tesla-ceo-elon-musk-says-he-was-raised-by-books.html

37 Berns, G.S, Blaine, K., Prietula, M.J, Pye, B.E. Short- and long-term effects of a novel on connectivity in the brain. Brain Connectivity, Vol3, No 6, 2013. Retrieved from https://www.ncbi.nlm.nih.gov/pubmed/23988110

38 Wagner, T. (2012). Creating Innovators: The making of young people who will change the world. Scribner, USA, 211.

39 Siraj-Blatchford, I. Creativity, Communication and Collaboration: The identification of pedagogic progression in sustained shared thinking. Asia-Pacific Journal of Research in Early Childhood Education, 2007, Vol.1, No.2, 3–23.

40 Imber, A. (2016) The Innovation Formula. John Wiley and Sons, Australia, 17.

41 Strong-Wilson, T, Ellis, J (2009) Children and Place: Reggio Emilia's Environment as Third Teacher. Theory into Practice Vol 46, 2007, Issue 1. Retrieved from https://www.lepetitgaulois.com/uploads/1/2/5/9/125913106/environment-as-the-3rd-teacher.pdf;
Carter, M. Making Your Environment 'The Third Teacher' Retrieved from https://www.lepetitgaulois.com/uploads/1/2/5/9/125913106/environment-as-the-3rd-teacher.pdf;
What is the Reggio Emilia philosophy? S=Scots College, Sydney. Retrieved from https://www.tsc.nsw.edu.au/tscnews/what-is-the-reggio-emilia-philosophy;
Reggio Emilia Australia Information Exchange website. Retrieved from https://reggioaustralia.org.au

42 Wagner, T. (2012). Creating Innovators: The making of young people who will change the world. Scribner, USA, 37–39, 137.

43 Grant, A. (2016) Originals: How non-conformists change the world. Penguin Random House, UK, 170–171.

44 Grant, A. (2016) Originals: How non-conformists change the world. Penguin Random House, UK, 172.

45 Bruce, M and Bridgeland, J. (2014) The Mentoring Effect: Young People's Perspectives on the Outcomes and Availability of Mentoring, Executive Summary. See also https://sites.sph.harvard.edu/wmy/national-mentoring-month/

46   Robinson, K. (2009) The Element: How finding your passion changes everything, Penguin USA, 179–183.

47   Robinson, K. (2009) The Element: How finding your passion changes everything, Penguin USA, 186.

48   Nielsen, D & Thurber, S (2016) The Secret of the Highly Creative Thinker. BIS Publishers, Netherlands, 45.

49   Kelley, T & Kelley. D. Creative Confidence Talks at Google. Nov 2013. Retrieved from https://www.youtube.com/watch?v=R_h1m9Njm_o

50   Gopnik, A. (2017) The Gardener and the Carpenter. Vintage Publishing, USA, 31.

51   Gopnik, A. In Defence of Play, Education, The Atlantic 12 August 2016. Retrieved from https://www.theatlantic.com/education/archive/2016/08/in-defense-of-play/495545/

52   Wagner, T. (2012). Creating Innovators: The making of young people who will change the world. Scribner, USA, 27.

53   Gopnik, A. In Defence of Play, Education, The Atlantic 12 August 2016. Retrieved from https://www.theatlantic.com/education/archive/2016/08/in-defense-of-play/495545/

54   Gopnik, A. Let the children play, It's good for them. Smithsonian Magazine July 2012. Retrieved from https://www.smithsonianmag.com/science-nature/let-the-children-play-its-good-for-them-130697324/

55   Gopnik, A. (2017) The Gardener and the Carpenter. Vintage Publishing, USA, 150-151; Gopnik, A. In Defence of Play, Education, The Atlantic 12 August 2016. Retrieved from https://www.theatlantic.com/education/archive/2016/08/in-defense-of-play/495545/

56   The Science of Creativity, Special Edition Time, March 2019, 70–74.

57   The Science of Creativity, Special Edition Time, March 2019, 73.

58   Gopnik, A. (2017) The Gardener and the Carpenter. Vintage Publishing, USA, 36.

59   Wang, C, Williams K.E, Shahaeian A, Harrison, L.J. Early predictors of escalating internalizing problems across middle childhood. Sch Psycol Q, 2018, June 33 (2): 200–212. Retrieved from https://www.ncbi.nlm.nih.gov/pubmed/28795830

60   DeWitt, P. Kids need play and Recess. Their mental health may depend on it. August 2018. Education Week. Retrieved from http://blogs.edweek.org/edweek/finding_common_ground/2018/08/the_existential_mental_health_crisis_in_k-12_education_the_need_for_play_and_recess.html?cmp=SOC-SHR-FB
If a person has an internal locus of control, that person attributes success to his or her own efforts and abilities. A person who expects to succeed will be more motivated and more likely to learn.

61   Danniels, E & Pyle, A. Defining play-based learning, Encyclopedia of early Childhood Development, Feb 2018, 1–3. Retrieved from http://www.child-encyclopedia.com/play-based-learning/according-experts/defining-play-based-learning

62   Toril, K. Fox, Dr S, Cloney, Dr D. Quality is the key in early childhood education in Australia. October 2017. Mitchell Institute Paper No 01/2017. Retrieved from http://www.mitchellinstitute.org.au/wp-content/uploads/2017/10/Quality-is-key-in-early-childhood-education-in-Australia.pdf

63   Yogman, M et al. The Power of Play: A Paediatric Role in Enhancing Development in Young Children. Pediatrics, Sept 2018. Retrieved from https://pediatrics.aappublications.org/content/142/3/e20182058.short;

64   UN Convention on the rights of children. Retrieved from http://ipaworld.org/childs-right-to-play/uncrc-article-31/un-convention-on-the-rights-of-the-child-1/

65   Robinson, K. (2011). Out of Our Minds: Learning to be Creative. Capstone Publishing, UK, 8.

66   The Science of Creativity, Special Edition Time, March 2019, 85.

67   Kim, K.H. The Creativity Crisis: the decrease in creative thinking scores on the Torrance tests of creative thinking. Abstract, Creativity Research Journal, Vol 23, 2011, Issue 4. Retrieved from https://www.tandfonline.com/doi/abs/10.1080/10400419.2011.627805
USA statistic – The decrease in creativity scores for kindergartners through third graders was the most significant.

68   Robinson, K. (2011). Out of Our Minds: Learning to be Creative. Capstone Publishing, UK, 266–267.

69   Gopnik, A. What is my child thinking? All in the Mind. February 2020. Retrieved from https://www.abc.net.au/radionational/programs/allinthemind/what-is-my-child-thinking/11909876

70   The Science of Creativity, Special Edition Time, March 2019, 85.

71 The Science of Creativity, Special Edition Time, March 2019, 87.
72 Finland was ranked third in 2019, up from 7th in 2018 in Bloomberg Innovation Index and 6th in Global Innovation index. Retrieved from https://www.globalinnovationindex.org/gii-2019-report#
73 Wagner, T. (2012). Creating Innovators: The making of young people who will change the world. Scribner, USA, 199.
74 Wagner, T. (2012). Creating Innovators: The making of young people who will change the world. Scribner, USA, 199–200.
75 Lord, R. What can we learn from Finland's education system? May 2018. Retrieved from https://hk.asiatatler.com/life/finland-education-system
76 Jezzard, A. Is the Finnish school the perfect design? October 2017. World Economic Forum. Retrieved from https://www.weforum.org/agenda/2017/10/why-finland-is-tearing-down-walls-in-schools/
77 Note the Early Years Learning Framework, Discussion Papers, Dept of Education, Skills and Employment, Australian Government. Retrieved from https://www.education.gov.au/early-years-learning-framework-0
78 Gopnik, A. (2017) The Gardener and the Carpenter. Vintage Publishing, USA, 197.
79 Grant, A. (2016) Originals: How non-conformists change the world. Penguin Random House, UK, 10.
80 Wagner, T. (2012). Creating Innovators: The making of young people who will change the world. Scribner, USA, 200.
81 Curriculum connections. The Australian Curriculum recognises the importance of play and outdoor learning.
Retrieved from https://www.australiancurriculum.edu.au/resources/curriculum-connections/
82 Wagner, T. (2012). Creating Innovators: The making of young people who will change the world. Scribner, USA, 25.
83 Wagner, T. (2012). Creating Innovators: The making of young people who will change the world. Scribner, USA, 56–58.
84 Wagner, T. (2012). Creating Innovators: The making of young people who will change the world. Scribner, USA, Adapted from Chapter 2.
85 Harvard and Stanford were ranked in the top 5 US universities in 2020. Retrieved from https://www.timeshighereducation.com/student/best-universities/best-universities-united-states
86 Maria Simonelli Understanding Organisational Creativity in Small- to Medium-Sized Enterprises: Does Size Matter? July 2016, Research thesis, Monash University.
87 Pink, D. (2005) A Whole New Mind: Moving from the information age to the conceptual age. Allen and Unwin, Australia, 131. Daniel Pink quoting designer Clement Mok and referencing Mihalyi Csikszentmilhalyi.
88 Amabile, T. (1997). Motivating Creativity in Organisations: On doing what you love and loving what you do. California Management Review, Vol. 40, No 1, Fall 1997, 45.r
89 Imber, A. (2016) The Innovation Formula. John Wiley and Sons, Australia, 31.
90 Amabile, T. (1997). Motivating Creativity in Organisations: On doing what you love and loving what you do. California Management Review, Vol. 40, No 1, Fall 1997, 45.r
91 Amabile, T. (1997). Motivating Creativity in Organisations: On doing what you love and loving what you do.
California Management Review, Vol. 40, No 1, Fall 1997, 39–58.
92 Burkus, D. (2014). The Myths of Creativity: The Truth About How Innovative Companies and People Generate Great Ideas. Jossey-Bass US.
93 Puccio, G. (2014) The Creative Thinker's Toolkit. The Great Courses, The Teaching Company, USA, 374;
Creative Climate Internal Conditions for Creative Behaviour and Performance Questionnaire by Goran Ekvall, 1996 Organizational climate for creativity and innovation. *European Journal of Work and Organizational Psychology*, 5 (1), 105–123. Retrieved from http://www.creativeproblemsolving.com/tools/creative_climate_ekvall.pdf
94 Puccio, G. (2014) The Creative Thinker's Toolkit. The Great Courses, The Teaching Company, USA, 375–379.
95 Adapted from Amabile, T & Khaire, M. Creativity and the Role of the Leader, Harvard Business Review, Oct 2008, 106–08; Amabile, T. (1997). Motivating Creativity in Organisations: On doing

what you love and loving what you do. California Management Review, Vol. 40, No 1, Fall 1997, 39–58.
96 Imber, A. (2016) The Innovation Formula. John Wiley and Sons, Australia, 4–5.
97 Imber, A. (2016) The Innovation Formula. John Wiley and Sons, Australia, 21.
98 Shalley, C.E. & Gilson, L.L. (2004). What leaders need to know: a review of social and contextual factors that can foster or hinder creativity. The Leadership Quarterly, Vol. 15, 33–53.
99 Amabile, T., Hadley C.N., & Kramer S.J., (2002). Creativity Under the Gun, Harvard Business Review, August 2002, 61.
Amabile, T & Khaire, M. Creativity and the Role of the Leader, Harvard Business Review, Oct 2008, 104.
100 Adapted from Amabile, T & Khaire, M. Creativity and the Role of the Leader, Harvard Business Review, Oct 2008, 107.
101 Adapted from Amabile, T & Khaire, M. Creativity and the Role of the Leader, Harvard Business Review, Oct 2008, 108.
102 Adapted from Amabile, T & Khaire, M. Creativity and the Role of the Leader, Harvard Business Review, Oct 2008, 102–109.
103 Driver, M. (2001). Fostering Creativity in Business Education: Developing Creative Classroom Environments to Provide Students with Critical Workplace Competencies. Journal of Education for Business, Sept–Oct 2001, 28–33.
104 Amabile, T., Schatzel, E.A., Moneta, G.B., Kramer, S.J. Leader behaviours and the work environment for creativity: Perceived leaders support. The Leadership Quarterly 15 (2004) 30.
105 Heffernan, M (2015) Beyond Measure: The Big Impact of Small Changes. Simon and Schuster, UK, 5.
106 Puccio, G. (2014) The Creative Thinker's Toolkit. The Great Courses, The Teaching Company, USA, 387.
107 Amabile, T. (1998) How to Kill Creativity. Harvard Business Review, Sept–Oct 199, 80. Based on 20 years of research by Professor Amabile.
108 Amabile, T. (1998) How to Kill Creativity. Harvard Business Review, Sept–Oct 1998, 81.
109 Imber, A. (2016) The Innovation Formula. John Wiley and Sons, Australia, 19;
Amabile, T. (1998) How to Kill Creativity. Harvard Business Review, Sept–Oct 1998, 82.
110 Amabile, T., Hadley C.N., & Kramer S.J., (2002). Creativity Under the Gun, Harvard Business Review, August 2002, 52–61.
111 Burkus, D. (2013) The Myths of Creativity, John Wiley and Sons, USA, 165.
112 Imber, A. (2016) The Innovation Formula. John Wiley and Sons, Australia, 99–102.
113 Maria Simonelli Understanding Organisational Creativity in Small- to Medium-Sized Enterprises: Does Size Matter? July 2016, Research thesis, submitted Monash University, 33.
114 Heffernan, M (2015) Beyond Measure: The Big Impact of Small Changes. Simon and Schuster, UK, 44.
115 Heffernan, M (2015) Beyond Measure: The Big Impact of Small Changes. Simon and Schuster, UK, 9.
116 Burkus, D. (2013) The Myths of Creativity, John Wiley and Sons, USA, 149.
117 Imber, A. (2016) The Innovation Formula. John Wiley and Sons, Australia, 47;
Amabile, T. (1998) How to Kill Creativity. Harvard Business Review, Sept–Oct 1998, 83.
118 Leonard, D. & Straus, S. Putting your company's whole brain to work. Harvard Business Review July–August 1997, 63.
119 Seeleg, T. (2012) Ingenius: A crash course in creativity. Harper Collins, USA, 146.
120 Amabile, T. (1998) How to Kill Creativity. Harvard Business Review, Sept–Oct 1998, 83.
121 Seeleg, T. (2012) Ingenius: A crash course in creativity. Harper Collins, USA, 120.
122 Shalley, C.E. & Gilson, L.L. (2004). What leaders need to know: a review of social and contextual factors that can foster or hinder creativity. The Leadership Quarterly, Vol. 15, 33–53.
123 Amabile, T. (1998) How to Kill Creativity. Harvard Business Review, Sept–Oct 1998, 84.
124 Imber, A. (2016) The Innovation Formula. John Wiley and Sons, Australia, 94.
125 Harford, T. (2016) Messy: How to creative and resilient in a tidy minded world. Abacus, UK, 52.
126 Harford, T. (2016) Messy: How to creative and resilient in a tidy minded world. Abacus, UK, 57.
127 Harford, T. (2016) Messy: How to creative and resilient in a tidy minded world. Abacus, UK, 62–64.

128 Mumford, M.D, Scott, G.M, Gaddis, B, Strange, J.M. Leading Creative People: Orchestrating expertise and relationships. The Leadership Quarterly, 13 (2002), 705.

129 Mumford, M.D, Scott, G.M, Gaddis, B, Strange, J.M. Leading Creative People: Orchestrating expertise and relationships. The Leadership Quarterly, 13 (2002), 719.

130 Puccio, G. (2014) The Creative Thinker's Toolkit. The Great Courses, The Teaching Company, USA, 392.

131 Puccio, G. (2014) The Creative Thinker's Toolkit. The Great Courses, The Teaching Company, USA, 393.

132 Nikravan, L. Why creativity is the most important leadership quality. May 2012, Chief Learning Officer. Retrieved from https://www.chieflearningofficer.com/2012/05/30/why-creativity-is-the-most-important-leadership-quality/

133 Adapted from Amabile, T & Khaire, M. Creativity and the Role of the Leader, Harvard Business Review, Oct 2008, 106–7;
Leonard, D. & Straus, S. Putting your company's whole brain to work. Harvard Business Review July–August 1997, 63;
Pink, D. (2011). Drive: The Surprising Truth About What Motivates Us. Penguin, USA, 162–167. Not sure where your organisation is at on the creativity-innovation spectrum? Try taking a quick snapshot via Innovation Culture Audit to determine how your organisation performs across a number of dimensions including the individual, team, leader and organisational level factors. Go to The Innovation Formula, Dr Amantha Imber for more science-based approaches to improving the innovation output of your organisation. Imber, A. (2016) The Innovation Formula. John Wiley and Sons, Australia.

134 Kaufman, S.B. The creative life and well-being. Scientific American, March 2015. Retrieved from https://blogs.scientificamerican.com/beautiful-minds/the-creative-life-and-well-being/

135 Richards, R. Everyday Creativity, Process and way of life – four key issues. Chapter 10 from Kaufman, J.C and Sternberg R.J (2011) The Cambridge Handbook of Creativity, Cambridge University Press, UK, 29.

136 Richards, R. Everyday Creativity, Process and way of life – four key issues. Chapter 10 from Kaufman, J.C and Sternberg R.J (2011) The Cambridge Handbook of Creativity, Cambridge University Press, UK, 192.

137 Kaufman, S.B. The creative life and well-being. Scientific American, March 2015. Retrieved from https://blogs.scientificamerican.com/beautiful-minds/the-creative-life-and-well-being/,

138 Richards, R. Everyday Creativity, Process and way of life – four key issues. Chapter 10 from Kaufman, J.C and Sternberg R.J (2011) The Cambridge Handbook of Creativity, Cambridge University Press, UK, 193.

139 Abraham Harold Maslow, Retrieved from https://en.wikipedia.org/wiki/Abraham_Maslow

140 McLeod, S. (2018) Maslow's Hierarchy of Needs, Simply Psychology. Retrieved from https://www.simplypsychology.org/maslow.html

141 Csikszentmihalyi, M. Quote re flow. Retrieved from https://www.verywellmind.com/what-is-flow-2794768

142 McLeod, S. (2018) Maslow's Hierarchy of Needs, Simply Psychology. Retrieved from https://www.simplypsychology.org/maslow.html

143 Deci, E.L & and Ryan, R.M. Hedonia, eudaimonia, and well-being: an introduction, Journal of Happiness Studies, January 2008, Volume 9, Issue 1, pp 1–11 Retrieved from https://link.springer.com/article/10.1007/s10902-006-9018-1#page-1

144 Kaufman, S.B. The creative life and well-being. Scientific American, March 2015. Retrieved from https://blogs.scientificamerican.com/beautiful-minds/the-creative-life-and-well-being/

145 Dodge, R. Daly, A. Huyton. J., Sanders L.D., The challenge of defining wellbeing. International Journal of Wellbeing, 2(3) 222–235. Retrieved from https://www.internationaljournalofwellbeing.org/index.php/ijow/article/view/89

146 Pink, D. (2011) Drive: the surprising truth about what motivates us. Penguin Putnam, USA, 80–81.

147 Swart, T. (2019) The Source: Open your mind, Change your life. Penguin Random House, UK, 159.

148 The Inventory of Strengths is designed to identify an individual's profile of character strengths and was designed by Christopher Peterson and Martin Seligman. The VIA (Values in Action) Inventory of Strengths is a measure of character strengths and a survey is available online, over 400,000 people have participated so far. They have published the Character Strengths and Virtues: A Handbook and Classification, Peterson and Seligman (2004). Retrieved from https://en.wikipedia.org/wiki/Values_in_Action_Inventory_of_Strengths

149 Pink, D. (2011) Drive: the surprising truth about what motivates us. Penguin Putnam, USA, 207–208

150 Not sure about your why? Check out Simon Sinek TED talk to learn more. Retrieved from https://www.ted.com/talks/simon_sinek_how_great_leaders_inspire_action

151 McKay, S. The Neuroscience Academy Lecture series, Applied Science and Brain Health. Retrieved from http://theneuroacademy.com Lecture 11; Swart, T. (2019) The Source: Open your mind, Change your life. Penguin Random House, UK, 159.
The Blue Zones research has identified locations where people reach the age of one hundred years at rates ten times greater than elsewhere in the world and usually in exceptional good health.

152 Pink, D. (2011) Drive: the surprising truth about what motivates us. Penguin Putnam, USA, Chapters 4,5,6;
Dean, B. Series Introduction, Authentic Happiness, Penn University. Retrieved from https://www.authentichappiness.sas.upenn.edu/newsletters/authentichappinesscoaching/creativity

153 Pink, D. (2011) Drive: the surprising truth about what motivates us. Penguin Putnam, USA, 122–25.

154 Hickie, I & Randles, J. Knitting your way to a healthier, happier mind. The Conversation, September 11, 2015. Retrieved from https://theconversation.com/knitting-your-way-to-a-healthier-happier-mind-46389

155 Luckman, S. How craft is good for our health, The Conversation, July 27, 2018 Retrieved from https://theconversation.com/how-craft-is-good-for-our-health-98755

156 Luckman, S. How craft is good for our health, The Conversation, July 27, 2018 Retrieved from https://theconversation.com/how-craft-is-good-for-our-health-98755

157 Kaimal, G. Ray, K. & Muniz, J. Reduction of Cortisol Levels and Participant's' Responses Following Art Making, 23 May 2016, Journal of the American Art Therapy Association.
Retrieved from https://www.tandfonline.com/doi/full/10.1080/07421656.2016.1166832

158 McKay, S. The Neuroscience Academy Lecture series, Applied Science and Brain Health. Retrieved from http://theneuroacademy.com Lecture 16

159 McKay, S. The Neuroscience Academy Lecture series, Applied Science and Brain Health. Retrieved from http://theneuroacademy.com Lecture 16

160 Lesser, C. Why Your Doctor May Be Prescribing Art Classes in the Future, Sep 19, 2018, Artsy. Retrieved from https://www.artsy.net/article/artsy-editorial-doctor-prescribing-art-classes-future; Solly, M. British Doctors May Soon Prescribe Art, Music, Dance, Singing Lessons, November 8, 2018, Smithsonian magazine. Retrieved from https://www.smithsonianmag.com/smart-news/british-doctors-may-soon-prescribe-art-music-dance-singing-lessons-180970750/#gfXRi8KdFT2s-WFQH.99;
Matt Hancock, MP from West Suffolk, Social Prescribing Speech 6 November 2018. Retrieved from https://www.matt-hancock.com/news/social-prescribing-speech

161 Stuckey, H. Nobel, J. The Connection Between Art, Healing and Public Health: A review of current literature. Framing Health Matters. American Journal of Public Health, Feb 2010, Vol 100, No. 2.

162 Tudor, R. Maidment, J. Campbell, A, Whittaker, K. Examining the Role of Craft in Post-Earthquake Recovery: Implications for Social Work Practice, British Journal of Social Work Dec 2015, Vol 45, Issue Suppl_1
Retrieved from https://academic.oup.com/bjsw/article-abstract/45/suppl_1/i205/2472333

163 Hickie, I & Randles, J. Knitting your way to a healthier, happier mind. The Conversation, September 11, 2015. Retrieved from https://theconversation.com/knitting-your-way-to-a-healthier-happier-mind-46389

164 Luckman, S. How craft is good for our health, The Conversation, July 27, 2018 Retrieved from https://theconversation.com/how-craft-is-good-for-our-health-98755

165 Luckman, S. How craft is good for our health, The Conversation, July 27, 2018 Retrieved from https://theconversation.com/how-craft-is-good-for-our-health-98755

166 Clave-Brule, M. Mazloum, A Park, R.J, Birmingham, C.L. Managing anxiety in eating disorders with knitting. Eat Weight Disorder 2009, March; 14 (1) e 1–5.
Retrieved from https://www.ncbi.nlm.nih.gov/pubmed/19367130

167 The Health Benefits of Knitting, Produced by Knit for Peace, summary, 3. Retrieved from https://knitforpeace.org.uk/knit-for-good/the-health-benefits-of-knitting

168 Westheimer, O. McRae, C. Henchcliffe, A. Fesharaki, A. Glazman, S. Ene, H. Bodis-Wollner, I. Dance for PD: a preliminary investigation of effects on motor function and quality of life amongst persons with Parkinson's disease (PD). 3 April 2015. J Neural Transm (2015) 122: 1263–1270.
Retrieved from http://danceforparkinsons.org/resources/research

169 Culph, J.S. Wilson N.J. Cordier, R. Stancliffe, R.J. Men's Sheds and the Experience of Depression in

170   Older Australian men. Australian Occupational Therapy Journal 2015 Oct, 62 (5): 306–15. Retrieved from https://www.ncbi.nlm.nih.gov/pubmed/26061865

170   Culph, J.S. Wilson N.J. Cordier, R. Stancliffe, R.J. Men's Sheds and the Experience of Depression in Older Australian men. Australian Occupational Therapy Journal 2015 Oct, 62 (5): 306–15. Retrieved from https://www.ncbi.nlm.nih.gov/pubmed/26061865

171   Tyler, C. (lead) Art Creativity and Learning, Final Workshop Report June 11–13 2008 National Science Foundation Report. Retrieved from https://www.arts.gov/publications/how-creativity-works-brain

172   Posner, M. Patoine, B. How Arts Training Improves Attention and Cognition, September 14, 2009, Cerebrum Dana Foundation. Retrieved from https://www.dana.org/article/how-arts-training-improves-attention-and-cognition

173   Posner, M. Patoine, B. How Arts Training Improves Attention and Cognition, September 14, 2009, Cerebrum Dana Foundation. Retrieved from https://www.dana.org/article/how-arts-training-improves-attention-and-cognition

174   The Mayo Clinic is an American not-for-profit organisation and academic medical centre focused on integrated clinical practice, education and research.

175   Can arts, crafts and computer use preserve your memory? Press Release, American Academy of Neurology. April, 2015. Retrieved from https://www.aan.com/PressRoom/Home/PressRelease/1363

176   Eagleman, D., Brandt, A (2017) The Runaway Species: How human creativity remakes the world. Canongate, UK, 186.

177   These are the areas of decline according to Seligman, M. Foreman, M & Kaufman, S.C. Creativity and Aging: What we can make with what we have left. March 2016. Retrieved from https://www.semanticscholar.org/paper/11-Creativity-and-Aging-%3A-What-We-Can-Make-With-We-Seligman-Forgeard/1669951df3c51d02cc68aaab9bd3b8d9a8acdb47

178   McKay, S. The Neuroscience Academy Lecture series, Applied Science and Brain Health. Retrieved from http://theneuroacademy.com Lecture 17.

179   McKay, S. The Neuroscience Academy Lecture series, Applied Science and Brain Health. Retrieved from http://theneuroacademy.com Lecture 17.

180   Seligman, M. Foreman, M & Kaufman, S.C. Creativity and Aging: What we can make with what we have left. March 2016. Retrieved from https://www.semanticscholar.org/paper/11-Creativity-and-Aging-%3A-What-We-Can-Make-With-We-Seligman-Forgeard/1669951df3c51d02cc68aaab9bd3b8d9a8acdb47

181   Seligman, M. Foreman, M & Kaufman, S.C. Creativity and Aging: What we can make with what we have left. March 2016. Retrieved from https://www.semanticscholar.org/paper/11-Creativity-and-Aging-%3A-What-We-Can-Make-With-We-Seligman-Forgeard/1669951df3c51d02cc68aaab9bd3b8d9a8acdb47

182   Levitin, D (2020) The Changing Mind: A Neuroscientist's Guide to Ageing Well, Penguin Random House, UK, 25–26.

183   Daniel Levitin, Professor of Psychology and Neuroscience at Macgill University in Montreal. Interview All in the Mind, April 2020 Retrieved from https://www.abc.net.au/radionational/programs/allinthemind/the-ageing-brain:-it-aint-all-downhill/12125478

184   Levitin, D (2020) The Changing Mind: A Neuroscientist's Guide to Ageing Well, Penguin Random House, UK, 173.

185   Levitin, D (2020) The Changing Mind: A Neuroscientist's Guide to Ageing Well, Penguin Random House, UK, 173–4.

186   Levitin, D (2020) The Changing Mind: A Neuroscientist's Guide to Ageing Well, Penguin Random House, UK, 285.

187   The Science of Creativity, Special Edition Time, March 2019, 80.

188   The Science of Creativity, Special Edition Time, March 2019, 80–81.

189   The Science of Creativity, Special Edition Time, March 2019, 80–81.

190   Galenson, D. (2009) Conceptual Revolutions in Twentieth-Century Art. Cambridge Uni Press, UK. David Galenson is a professor at the University of Chicago.

191   Galenson, D. (2009) Conceptual Revolutions in Twentieth-Century Art. Cambridge Uni Press, UK, 107.

192   Galenson, D. (2009) Conceptual Revolutions in Twentieth-Century Art. Cambridge Uni Press, UK, 9.

193 Galenson, D & Clayne, P. (2013) Abstract retrieved from https://www.tandfonline.com/doi/abs/10.1080/01615440.2012.719427

194 Galenson, D. (2009) Conceptual Revolutions in Twentieth-Century Art. Cambridge Uni Press, UK, 82.

195 Grant, A. (2016) Originals: How non-conformists change the world. Penguin Random House, UK, 110.

196 Grant, A. (2016) Originals: How non-conformists change the world. Penguin Random House, UK, 110.

197 Grant, A. (2016) Originals: How non-conformists change the world. Penguin Random House, UK, 110.

198 Grant, A. (2016) Originals: How non-conformists change the world. Penguin Random House, UK, 110.

199 Grant, A. (2016) Originals: How non-conformists change the world. Penguin Random House, UK, 111.

200 Seligman, M. Foreman, M & Kaufman, S.C. Creativity and Aging: What we can make with what we have left. March 2016, 344. Retrieved from https://www.semanticscholar.org/paper/11-Creativity-and-Aging-%3A-What-We-Can-Make-With-We-Seligman-Forgeard/1669951d-f3c51d02cc68aaab9bd3b8d9a8acdb47

201 Check appendix 1 for answers

202 Robinson, K. (2011) Out of Our Minds: Learning to be creative, Capstone publishing Ltd, UK, 286.

203 *Lone creator* is one of many myths coined by Burkus, D. (2014). The Myths of Creativity: The Truth About How Innovative Companies and People Generate Great Ideas. Jossey-Bass US.

204 Robinson, K. (2011) Out of Our Minds: Learning to be creative, Capstone publishing Ltd, UK, xvii.

205 Robinson, K. (2011) Out of Our Minds: Learning to be creative, Capstone publishing Ltd, UK, xvii.

206 Gelb, M. (2014) Creativity on Demand: how to ignite and sustain the fire of genius. Sounds True, USA, xvii

207 Csikszentmihalyi, M. Creativity across the life-span: A systems view. Talent Development III, Gifted Psychology Press, 1995, 9–18. Retrieved from https://www.davidsongifted.org/search-database/entry/a10009

208 Csikszentmihalyi, M. Creativity across the life-span: A systems view. Talent Development III, Gifted Psychology Press, 1995, 9–18. Retrieved from https://www.davidsongifted.org/search-database/entry/a10009

209 https://www.davidsongifted.org/search-database/entry/a10009

210 Grant, A. (2016) Originals: How non-conformists change the world. Penguin Random House, UK, 108–113.

211 Dweck, C. (2012). Mindset: How You Can Fulfil Your Potential. Little Brown Book Group, UK, 6. Pdf version

212 Dweck, C. (2012). Mindset: How You Can Fulfil Your Potential. Little Brown Book Group, UK, 6. Pdf version

213 Dweck, C. (2012). Mindset: How You Can Fulfil Your Potential. Little Brown Book Group, UK, 7–8. Pdf version

214 Studies compiled in *The Cambridge Handbook of Expertise and Expert Performance, published* by Cambridge University Press 2006 and edited by K. Anders Ericsson. K. Anders Ericsson is a Swedish psychologist and Conradi Eminent Scholar and Professor of Psychology at Florida State University who is internationally recognised as a researcher in the psychological nature of expertise and human performance.

215 Ericsson, A.K, Prietula, M.J, Cokely, E.T. (2007). The Making of an Expert, Harvard Business Review. Retrieved from https://hbr.org/2007/07/the-making-of-an-expert

216 Ericsson, A and Pool, R, (2016). Peak: Secrets from the new science of expertise. Penguin Random House, UK, 14–22.

217 Colvin, G. (2012). Talent is Overrated: What really separates world-class performers from everybody else. John Murray Press, UK, 94.

218 Mandell, F & Jordan, K. (2010) Becoming a Life Change Artist: Seven creative skills to reinvent yourself at any stage of your life. Penguin Group, USA

219 This framework was successfully utilised in the Sweet Spot Careers book to support midlife professionals make sensible career and life transitions. You'll find a similar set of skills in the work by innovation author Gelb, M.J. (1998) How to Think Like Leonardo da Vinci. Bantell Dell, USA.

220 Linkner, J (2011) Disciplined Dreaming: A proven system to drive breakthrough creativity. USA, Jossey-Bass, 28. Quote attributed to Hal Gregersen, Professor at INSEAD business school.

www.ingramcontent.com/pod-product-compliance
Lightning Source LLC
Chambersburg PA
CBHW080847020526
44107CB00079B/2632